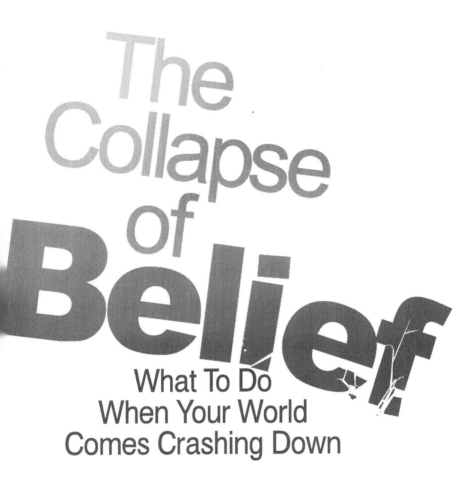

The Collapse of Belief

What To Do When Your World Comes Crashing Down

The Collapse of Belief

What To Do When Your World Comes Crashing Down

Kurt Hanks and Barbara Hanks

Illustrated by Kurt Hanks

www.collapseofbelief.com

ISBN-13: 978-1456419516
© 2012 Kurt Hanks and Barbara Hanks

CONTENTS

1   **When Your Life Turns Upside Down** 9
    Lose Your Beliefs—Lose Your Way

2   **The Belief Window** 15
    *It Determines What You See or Don't See—
What You Do or Don't Do*

3   **Beliefs Box You In** 27
    *Beliefs Set The Boundaries of
Your Interactions and Exchanges*

4   **Ties That Blind** 37
    Relationships Confirm Your Beliefs

5   **Locking The Box Shut** 47
    *Contradiction of a Belief
Leads to Manipulation and Projection*

6   **When the Box Collapses** 55
    Two Ways to Handle a Collapse of Belief

7   **Conscious Believing** 63
    Changing Your Beliefs about Beliefs

8   **Redefining Your Defining Beliefs** 71
    *Up From the Basement, Out Into the Light,
and Onto the Table*

9   **The Secret Is In The Relationship** 79
    *Discerning the Belief Driving an
Exchange Always Changes You*

10   **Beyond Belief** 89

    Acknowledgments 99

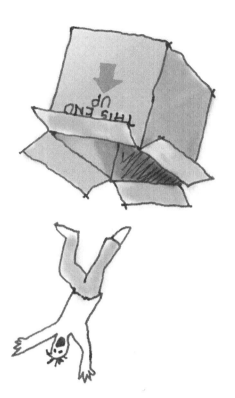

1
When Your Life Turns Upside Down

It was 11:30 on a winter night, and someone was pounding on the front door. I stumbled out of bed to find my friend Kerry standing ashen-faced on the porch. As I pulled him in out of the cold, his words tumbled over one another: "It can't be true, Kurt! It just can't be!"

"What can't be true?" I asked. Collapsing on the couch, Kerry blurted out the story his brother had told him that day: "Craig said Joseph Smith married other men's wives. I didn't believe him, so I looked at the Church's geneological records on the Internet. It showed that the prophet not only married women who were already married, he also married young girls—a lot of them! Some as young as fourteen!" Kerry looked at me with a tortured expression. "Kurt, that's one of the characteristics of a cult—the leader feels entitled to everyone's wives!" Kerry slumped over, cradling his head in his hands.

My first instinct was to say, "Well, where have *you* been? That information's been available for decades." But I thought better of it, seeing his obvious distress. What he needed now was comfort, not chiding.

With this devastating revelation, my friend's belief in the divinely-inspired, selfless founder of the Mormon religion, to which he had devoted his entire life, was shaken to the core. Kerry sat

The Collapse of Belief

distraught and trembling on my sofa as I tried to help him come to terms with this life-altering information.

I have witnessed similar scenarios many times in my life: confused and overwhelmed people struggling with the collapse of a belief, whether it is religious, political, scientific, social, financial, or even their faith in themselves. Those experiences, along with our personal collapses, are what drove Barbara and me to write this book. In addition to our own suffering, our hearts have gone out over and over to friends and relatives who have invested their entire lives in a certain idea, relationship, philosophy or organization, only to discover that their conviction was built on a foundation of sand.

I'll never forget Tamara, sitting numb in the funeral of her barely-middle-aged husband. Her whole belief about her future collapsed at his death. Or Bob, a successful businessman, whose career inexplicably nose-dived after his divorce. Harold, another friend, described his loss of faith in his religion as the most painful experience he had ever gone through—even worse than the death of his wife or two bouts with cancer himself.

WHAT ARE BELIEFS, REALLY?

Beliefs saturate our lives, and people proclaim them all the time: "I believe in a strong America;" "I believe God will help me if I'm righteous;" "I believe in the scientific method;" "I believe my son would never do that," etc. Some beliefs are valid indicators of truth and some aren't, but that doesn't really matter; whether they are correct or not, *our beliefs become our reality*. We might believe that a good education ensures a comfortable lifestyle, or that if we file our taxes properly we will never be audited by the IRS. We might believe that if we follow all the rules of our religion we'll go to heaven, or we may think that someone at the front of a line has the right to be served next.

Whatever our beliefs are, when they are contradicted we become confused and bewildered, maybe even angry. The most powerful beliefs we have—what I call defining beliefs or governing paradigms—are those that define who we are and how our life works. They drive all our behavior: *This is how* this *works; when I do* this, that *happens; my life is on track because I've built it on a solid foundation of (fill in the blank)*.

As a defining belief collapses, the pain and frustration we experience can seem unbearable. We feel as though we're losing the very definition of who we are. Everything we knew for sure has suddenly disintegrated. Nothing is ever the same again. We are lost and wandering in a strange land.

When your life is functioning to your satisfaction, you take your beliefs for granted. You may not even know they exist or that they influence you. But what happens when your life doesn't work anymore? What do you do when things that used to flow successfully, somehow stop?

Well, you may find yourself living the definition of insanity: frantically doing the same thing over and over (because it used to work) expecting a different result than the one you're currently getting.

When you reach this point, nothing makes sense anymore. What you have always known cannot explain where you are now or where you're heading. The formulas you faithfully followed to create value in your life are useless. A friend of ours described it this way: "When I was younger, everything I touched turned to gold. Now, for some strange reason, I can't make anything work." Another friend, who is leaving a fundamentalist religion, said: "I feel like I'm falling off a cliff. Then I hit a ledge and regroup, but before long it collapses, and I fall again."

LOSE YOUR BELIEFS–LOSE YOUR WAY
When you lose the beliefs that explain your world—and even your definition of yourself—you lose your way. It's like standing in front of a map of your life, but you can't find the you-are-here arrow. Without a reference point, it's impossible to identify your position or plot a route to take you where you want to go. Your

The Collapse of Belief

sense of disorientation and powerlessness could also be described—as it was by one person we know—as being on the ocean in a rowboat with no oars.

You may also experience another problem: Even though you have lost your footing, those around you haven't lost theirs. While *your* beliefs have turned to mush, theirs remain solid. This may result in tension between you—even hostility. Your loss of belief threatens their comfortable, predictable world, and in order to maintain their equilibrium they may brand you as crazy, evil or irrelevant. The conflict between these two differing world views is one of the devastating consequences of the collapse of belief.

Because you're reading this book you're probably having some kind of a crisis of belief. Your world may be changing rapidly and inexorably, and you don't know how to put it back together—or even if you should. You're finding it impossible to function in life using the tools you're familiar with. So you fall.

Our friend Kerry, who was distraught over the information he had stumbled upon about his church's history, had a difficult time assimilating those new facts into his life. He struggled for years to come to terms with it, facing at the same time the collapse of several other dearly-held suppositions. With knowledge comes responsibility, and unfortunately, Kerry couldn't face the consequences of acting on his new-found awareness. He finally found a way to opt out of this life rather than go on the unfamiliar journey that was being offered to him.

But we have known many others who face the collapse of belief with courage and faith—trusting that when they act from a basis of their new understanding, things will somehow work out. We have seen parents and siblings of a gay child completely reverse their thinking about homosexuality when the horror of denying the humanity of their loved one is presented to them by clueless people and organizations. We have watched a newly-divorced mother, who had believed her marriage was forever, bravely pick up the pieces of her shattered life and make the best of a new belief system that felt upside-down.

You may be having the experience of looking back over the years and realizing that your entire approach to life has been defective, maybe even counterproductive. What do you do now?

A SUGGESTION
To survive and eventually thrive in the chaos and trauma of extreme change, you need a new belief about *beliefs*. You need to know what they are—and what they are not. You need to understand the strength beliefs give us, *and* their innate flaws. You also need to know how beliefs are created. When you become conscious of your belief-generating process, you can take more responsibility for your resulting choices. You will then have more power to navigate the turbulent waters of rapidly-changing and even collapsing beliefs.

At no time in your upbringing were you probably ever taught about beliefs, per se. You were most likely taught *what* to believe, but nothing about the nature of beliefs themselves.

Throughout this book we will build an observation point outside your belief structures. We'll show you what they really are, how you created them, how they work, and we'll give you an effective process to rebuild your life in the wake of their catastrophic loss. Then we'll take you beyond the collapse to the new world you are being invited into—one that may bring growth beyond anything you could have imagined.

How we perceive our world and respond to it is governed by the beliefs written on our Window.

The Belief Window

I made a unique discovery when I worked with a certain multi-millionaire. I had dealings with him on an occasional basis for years, and over all that time, he exhibited a lot of bizarre behavior. In the early years—before he made his money—his associates thought he was weird, but after he became rich, he was *eccentric.* With a laugh and a shrug, people explained his odd conduct as sunspot activity or tight shorts.

Then one day, while attending a meeting with this man, I suddenly understood the reason for his strange behavior. With a flash of insight I saw that all his actions were a result of a belief he had about himself. It was as if that belief were hanging on a window in front of his face, and he looked at the world through it.

This is the principle I saw written on his window: *MY WAY IS THE **RIGHT** WAY, AND I SEE EVERYTHING ABSOLUTELY CORRECTLY.*

THE VALUE OF THIS INSIGHT
At the same moment, I saw my future and the disasters that awaited me if I continued to have business dealings with this man. I could also see the past, and the thread that tied those years of erratic behavior together into a consistent pattern.

I named the phenomenon I saw that day "The Belief Window"

and taught the concept to subsequent associates who have spread it across the world through training companies, books and speakers' bureaus.

As the years have gone by I've seen the power of understanding this single principle—that people's actions will always be congruent with what is written on their Belief Window. If your business partner, for instance, has *I Am Always Right* written on his window, when you disagree over marketing directions, who will have the only correct view? And if your company goes under, whose fault would he insist it has to be—his, or yours? As long as that principle is written on his Belief Window, can you ever have an equitable exchange with him?

You may have a friend or relative with *I Am Only Valuable if I am Serving* written on her window. She exhausts herself taking care of everyone—but doesn't take care of her own needs properly.

Having this insight has been a lifesaver for me economically. With the initial discovery that the patterns of my rich friend's behavior were all consistent with his governing belief, I broke off my business dealings with him. Later, I warned others who were involved with him. They all said: "Don't get so worked up; things are going to be just fine. You've got to be crazy not to go in with us."

Six months later, when their business venture went bankrupt, I heard a different tune: "Boy, I wish I'd listened to you! I thought you were nuts, but *I* was the crazy one."

Since I first discovered the Belief Window, I see it everywhere I look. Being aware of other people's Windows (and my own) has proven to be a great tool in dealing with life.

WHAT'S WRITTEN ON THE WINDOW IS EASY TO READ
To determine what a person's beliefs are, simply notice the patterns in their interactions with others. *A proclamation of belief* does not necessarily represent the governing principles that dominate a person's life—their *actions* do.

With my former business associate, all I had to do was watch how he acted in a variety of situations. His responses all matched his governing belief.

The three stories below illustrate how our Windows define our behavior and influence how we make decisions.

The Belief Window

THE HYPNOTIZED SINGER
A few years ago, I was astonished by what I saw at one of those traveling hypnotist shows. One particular man who had volunteered to be hypnotized was brought on stage and asked to sing before he was "put under." His voice was raspy, and he hesitantly got through the song even with the laughter of the crowd.

He was then hypnotized by the expert and told he was a world-famous singer about to give one of his finest performances—that he was in front of a huge audience who had paid over $50 each to hear him. He was then asked to sing again. The difference was dramatic. This time, he was quite good, and very pleasing to hear—not fifty dollars' worth, but still much better than I had anticipated.

ROBERT'S POSSESSIONS GIVE HIM AWAY
My friend Robert has the appearance of being a person of substance and means. He drives a BMW, wears British suits and Italian shoes, and just got back from a European vacation with his Swedish wife.

Robert's consistent behavior allows us to read some of the principles on his Belief Window. One of them seems to be: *My Value as a Person is Shown by the High-Class Possessions I Own.* Another is: *European Culture and Products are of the Highest Quality.*

By knowing these principles Robert has bought into, I can better understand why he does what he does, without letting these things (that don't really matter to me) get in the way of our friendship.

JOHN LOVES MARY LOVES JOHN
John learned love from a family where love was given unconditionally and freely. No matter what he did, his parents still loved him. His father once said, "Even if you killed someone, we would still love you when you're on the electric chair."

Mary learned love from a family where love was given conditionally. These words,

The Collapse of Belief

though never spoken out loud, were always present in family relationships: "We love you if you do what we want, but we don't love you if you go against our wishes."

John and Mary got together, fell in love, and were married. They often told each other "I love you," but John was puzzled by Mary's rejection of him when he didn't behave in the exact manner she proscribed. Their loving words were identical, but the beliefs written on their Windows were different.

CREATING A BELIEF WINDOW

Your defining beliefs are usually constructed early in life from the way you interpret situations and interactions. They are like puzzle pieces that come together to form a window to your world.

Situations that build a belief:

Parents tell you that you were an unplanned pregnancy.

Friends only let you come to the party if you have a boyfriend.

Grandparents constantly laud your sister's achievements and good looks.

A **pedophile** molests you and is not held accountable for his actions.

At **church** you are taught about the hell that awaits nonbelievers.

The pieces fit together to form your Belief Window.

18

The Belief Window

A STORY OF BUILDING A BELIEF

Karl created a belief about himself in his childhood when he was kicked out of the house at age four by his father. He remembers standing under the eaves, trying to get out of the rain, thinking there was something he needed to do to fix the situation. He subconsciously formed two powerful beliefs about himself at that time: 1. *I am Responsible for Not Having a Home*, and 2. *It's My Job to Change a Situation Over Which I Have No Power*.

Those interconnected beliefs influenced Karl all his life. He never realized where his insecurity about *home* came from until he started examining his belief-creating process.

Once he understood it, and realized those beliefs were based on a false premise—that he was somehow at fault for his childhood abuse—the issues largely went away.

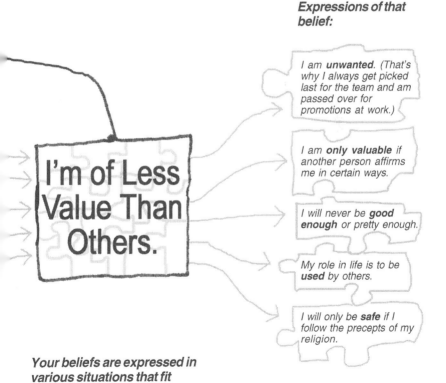

Expressions of that belief:

I am **unwanted**. *(That's why I always get picked last for the team and am passed over for promotions at work.)*

I am **only valuable** if another person affirms me in certain ways.

I will never be **good enough** or pretty enough.

My role in life is to be **used** by others.

I will only be **safe** if I follow the precepts of my religion.

Your beliefs are expressed in various situations that fit together to form your life.

The Collapse of Belief

The problem with inaccurately-formed beliefs is that they can lead you in the wrong direction. For example, a belief that the usual process of life won't provide for one's needs may justify stealing. A belief that there is nothing to live for can result in suicide.

But beliefs can be positive, too. A belief that you are competent and hard-working will lessen your anxiety in a new job. A belief that life is worth living motivates you to get up in the morning.

So beliefs can be rational and helpful, or totally illogical and destructive. They can encourage you to succeed, or cause you to make counterproductive and even disastrous decisions.

EXPRESSING WHAT IS WRITTEN ON YOUR BELIEF WINDOW

We can only operate from what is written on our Window, and we express our beliefs very clearly by our attitudes and actions. Many of our beliefs are not even conscious, but they still drive our decisions. Did you ever settle for less because you believed you weren't good enough or worthy of something better? Or conversely, was there a time you felt *too* good for a certain situation, then found out later it would have been perfect for you?

When you have a strong defining belief, you can actually *draw situations to you* that confirm your attitude about yourself. Here is a true story that illustrates that principle:

Chloe is a friend of Barbara's who was born in Italy during World War II, the love child of an English soldier and an Italian woman. After the war, when the serviceman went back to England and started another family, Chloe felt invisible to her father, who rarely contacted her. She created a Belief Window that stated, *I Am Invisible*, and to this day she carries such a strong energy of being unseen that people routinely treat her as if she isn't there.

For example, not long ago a car full of people with whom Chloe went to a seminar somehow left her behind at the end of the evening. No one in the vehicle, including Barbara, noticed she was missing. They were all horrified when they realized what they had done.

But the next day, at the continuation of the seminar, Chloe's background came out, and since Barbara was familiar with the Belief Window concept, she put it together. For the first time,

The Belief Window

she realized the power our beliefs carry. They not only affect our feelings and actions; they can even create a field around us that influences others.

GROUP BELIEF WINDOW
People often share the same Belief Window when they come together in groups. A shared Window is the commonality that binds them into a cohesive unit. Such groups can be formal or informal, and can consist of families, unions, companies, churches or even nations.

When looking through a single Belief Window, the group functions as one person.

The Collapse of Belief

SHARED WINDOWS

Here are examples of shared Belief Windows and the actions resulting from them:

NAZI GERMANY
Shared Belief Window: Man is a creature to be bred for quality to rule the world in a thousand-year reign.

Action: During the final battles of World War II, troop trains needed at the front were delayed so trains carrying "subhumans" to the concentration camps could get through.

MUSLIM EXTREMISTS
Shared Belief Window: Dying for the cause of Allah will take us directly to heaven.

Action: Devoted martyrs willingly die with bombs strapped to their bodies, killing many others in the process.

THE SMITH-JONES FAMILY
Shared Belief Window: Our family is more righteous and correct than any other.

Action: Bad things that happen in their family are blamed on someone else.

ACME COMPUTER COMPANY
Shared Belief Window: Customer service is our primary goal.

Action: Satisfied clients say, "It cost more for their equipment, but their customer service more than made up for it."

THE GOVERNMENT OF KING GEORGE III
Shared Belief Window: The Divine Right of Kings gives us the justification to enforce our will on everyone.

Action: Laws were imposed upon the American colonies.

THE AMERICAN COLONIES
Shared Belief Window: All men are created equal by God.

Action: Resistance to the king's imposition on the colonies led to the American Revolution.

MANY POLITICIANS
Shared Belief Window: We can hide our true motivations behind proclamations of serving our constituents.

Action: The political atmosphere is permeated with corruption and self-interest.

The Belief Window

REMINDER: As we stated on page 16, what is written on a person's or group's Window doesn't always match up with what they declare their beliefs to be. The key is to observe what they *do* more than what they *say*. It is not uncommon to read a Belief Window that is exactly opposite of what the owner asserts his or her beliefs are. I've typically found that the more a set of beliefs are promoted as a person's real beliefs, the more they are *not* the ones written on their Belief Window.

But sometimes they match. When you hear a friend say he believes in being kind, then you watch as he stays with a dying grandmother while everyone else abandons her to fight over her estate, you can be pretty certain your friend's Belief Window lines up with his publicly-stated values.

A UNIVERSAL PHENOMENON
The Belief Window is a naturally-occurring phenomenon for all humans. Everyone—from your nephew to the president of the United States—has an individually-constructed Window in front of them, and their lives are consistent with what they have written on its panes.

The more aware we are of our Windows, the more power we have to make sense of our lives. It allows us to explain past actions and even predict future behavior.

The Collapse of Belief

TOTAL INVESTMENT IN A SINGLE WINDOW
Here is a story about someone who didn't understand the nature of beliefs or the power they have over us:

Earl was a friend of mine who owned a bookstore. He loved to read and learn, and developed many strong beliefs, accompanied by very strong emotions.

When Earl felt passionately about something, he would back it up with everything he had. That's why, when he found himself in a heated dispute with another man, he didn't hesitate to get into a fist-fight.

The other guy socked Earl hard on the side of his face—so hard that a deep lesion developed, which eventually turned into cancer. He was told by doctors that the malignancy would be fatal if he didn't have it removed and treated properly.

Well, Earl's Belief Window said *I Am a Very Spiritual Man*, and he decided that God would heal him in a miraculous way. He didn't need the medical profession, or even any of those wacky alternative healing methods.

Besides, he didn't have the money to pay for treatment. He was positive that by his powerful faith and prayers, the Lord would get rid of the cancer. As he waited patiently for his miracle, the tumor grew until it distorted his face and jaw.

One day, while Earl was standing in line at a grocery store, the man behind him tapped him on the shoulder. He said he noticed the growth on Earl's face and that it looked like cancer. He went on to say that he was a plastic surgeon, and he could completely remove the growth and eradicate the disease.

Earl said he didn't have any money for medical treatment. The doctor said it didn't matter; he would do the surgery free of charge. And guess what Earl said next: "No thank you, I'm sure God is going to heal me."

You see, Earl had another, hidden, belief that was subordinate to the one listed above. It was *God Will Do Things My Way*. He wasn't consciously aware of that belief, but it drove most, if not all, of his actions.

A few months later, Earl's cancer became unbearably painful. He began throwing himself against the wall and even breaking furniture to ease his suffering. The pain finally overwhelmed his unrealistic belief in a miraculous cure, and he begged doctors for morphine. He eventually died a terrible, agonizing death.

Throughout Earl's life, he studied continually about *what* to believe, but he never studied *about* belief. He had no tools to deal with a contradiction to his deeply-held convictions. He didn't know that *beliefs are actually mental constructions we build to give meaning to our world.*

Earl's lack of understanding was essentially a death sentence for him—and it didn't need to be. I was so overcome with sadness at the senselessness of his passing I couldn't even go to his funeral. I felt his death was forced on him by his lack of knowledge. Nothing in his life had ever given him the ability to understand how to recognize or modify the beliefs on his Window. All he could do was go deeper and deeper into certainty.

MANY BELIEFS COME TO A VIOLENT END

You can see the violent collapse of belief in the world all around us—not only in personal stories like Earl's but in the relentless drama of human history. The events of 9/11 triggered the collapse of our belief about our invulnerability as a nation. The Iraq war ended our collective belief in the effectiveness of our country's intelligence-gathering capabilities, as well as the wisdom of our political leaders. In the recent economic downturn many lost their belief in Adam Smith's "invisible hand" of the free market that is supposed to turn self-interest into prosperity for all. History is littered with one monumental collapse after another.

We're always told to learn the lessons of the past. Maybe the biggest lesson we can learn is to become aware of our personal and cultural Belief Windows and how our total investment in them often leads to disaster.

It's our nature as humans to be believers and belief makers. When we are conscious of the process we use to build our Belief Windows, we can understand that they are merely creations of our mind. We get ourselves into trouble when we make beliefs absolutely real—when we imbue them with the aura of irrevocable truth. That's what makes their collapse unthinkable, and so incredibly painful.

We create a Box around our Belief Window consisting of interactions that validate what is written there.

Beliefs Box You In

People talk a lot about "thinking outside the box" or "getting out of the box," but you don't often hear what *The Box* actually is. For our purposes we will identify it as a structure formed by a defining belief. It contains all the interactions that validate or give expression to that belief. People inhabit a Box of their own or someone else's making if they buy in to the beliefs that created that Box.

Boxes can be built by individuals or groups. For example, the mortgage industry created a Box with this defining belief: *Real Estate Values Will Always Rise.* Bankers, Realtors, investors and home buyers were all enticed into that Box. The boundaries of all their exchanges were set by the solid walls of the Box that didn't allow any contradictory information in. Of the millions of investors and thousands of experts profiting from the housing bubble in the first decade of the 21st century, it is said that only about 20 market analysts recognized the signs of impending doom in the housing market and took advantage of the downturn.

Very few of us locked inside a Box can see beyond its walls—walls that make us blind and deaf to information that challenges our defining beliefs. The more firmly we adhere to those beliefs,

The Collapse of Belief

the more impermeable are the walls. Inside the Box, we mirror our beliefs to each other, ignoring any evidence that our beliefs might be false, or may need modifying.

BOXED IN—TO HEAR ONLY YOUR OWN VOICE

In the years leading up to the year 2000, as the Y2K hysteria started to take hold, I was associated with a group of businessmen who figured out a way to capitalize on the universal computer failure many people were convinced would occur as the clocks rolled over from 1999. This group was so sure society would implode on that date, they sank millions of dollars into land for a safe compound and bought massive amounts of food storage to sell for a profit to the anticipated desperate hordes of starving people.

Since I was consulting with this group at the time on another project, I was privy to some of their plans. I remember walking into a warehouse they had built, and looking incredulously at rows and rows of neatly-stacked boxes of emergency food supplies that reached from floor to ceiling.

The Box of their certainty had thick, impenetrable walls—all built on a single belief about the future and their destiny in dealing

with the coming disaster. They even had a high-powered adviser, a former vice president of AT&T, who assured them of the correctness of their vision. I watched from a distance as they amassed supplies and made elaborate plans for their lives in the new, chaotic environment they were positive was coming.

At one point I couldn't resist asking one of the principal developers what would happen if there was no gigantic computer collapse on January 1, 2000. He brushed me off, saying that *of course* it would happen. Well, you know the rest of the story. Nothing of any import happened on the first day of the new century.

But this is where the story gets more diabolical. It soon came out what this group had really been up to inside their Box. They had diverted funds entrusted to them from their clients—intended for legitimate investments—into solar-powered buildings and homes on their compound, as well as the stockpile of dehydrated food. They were so sure the world was going to collapse, they felt justified in embezzling all that money to protect themselves. They planned to use the food as leverage later to increase their holdings and pay back their investors.

The two main businessmen in this group were eventually indicted for fraud. One died before he went to jail, and the other spent some time in prison.

It's amazing to me the lengths people will go to in order to avoid peeking over the walls of their box.

ANOTHER IMPERMEABLE BOX

I seem to be a witness to tragic events that deal with unbending beliefs. One of the saddest scenarios, from a business standpoint, concerned a time-management company I once worked for that developed a popular planner several decades ago.

The defining belief they shared inside their box was *Our Product is Superior and Doesn't Need Changing.*

As technological advances were being made in the industry, the company managers tenaciously clung to their belief about the invincibility of their product line. I jointly ran the Research and Development department, and at one point I was given proposals by three different companies to replace our paper-oriented product with a digital one. I could see that the wave of the future in this field was electronic, so I strenuously recommended to

The Collapse of Belief

the upper management that they accept one of these offers. I showed them device after device as proposed prototypes, but they turned them all down. Their mantra was that there was only one true planner: it was paper and 5 ½ by 8 ½ .

Very soon thereafter, as electronic planners (PDAs) became more and more popular, this company's gross revenue went into a drastic decline—from half a *billion* dollars annually to $30 million, and their stock price went from over $50 per share to under a dollar. This chain of events is now a case study at Harvard Business School about what *not* to do in business.

The leadership of that corporation allowed it to slide into insignificance because they didn't recognize how deep into The Box they were. They were so intent on confirming to each other what was written on their shared Belief Window inside their Box, they ignored the changing world outside.

Since we all operate from the beliefs on our Window, our exchanges with others reflect those beliefs. When we force every exchange to conform to our beliefs, we strengthen the Box around us. As was stated above, only those people who concur with our view of ourselves and our world are allowed into our Box.

Sometimes the tenacity with which we reinforce the walls of our Box—even in the face of intense opposition—can land us in absurd situations. The cascading sequence of choices coming from a faulty belief can warp a person's behavior into something even they would have once considered grotesque, as can be seen in the following situation.

THE SOUL MATE BOX

Ellen is a divorced woman who is in love with a middle-aged man named Jack. She is absolutely sure they are destined to be together. In fact, Ellen recounts numerous spiritual experiences that led her to believe she and Jack are soul mates and have a glorious future, planned by God, to make an important impact on the planet.

Jack is a distinguished-looking man with a commanding presence who tells elaborate stories of his connections to worldwide financiers that are sure to bring him millions, if not billions, of dollars.

Ellen pursued Jack doggedly and convinced him, or so she thought, of their glorious future together. Jack lived in another city, but he visited Ellen often, staying overnight and assuring her she was his "one and only" and that they would be married soon. He also convinced Ellen to "invest" in his financial schemes to the tune of tens of thousands of dollars.

One day, Ellen hadn't heard from Jack for a while and was worried about him. Since he wasn't answering her calls, she thought he might be ill. She tracked down Jack's address and decided to drive the two hours to his home and make sure he was OK.

When she rang Jack's doorbell, she was greeted by his live-in girlfriend, Linda, whom Ellen knew nothing about. Jack just happened to be in a ten-year relationship about which he had neglected to inform his "one true love."

Ellen was shocked, but not deterred. She put tremendous pressure on Jack to forsake his lover and marry her as he had promised. Jack swore he would—as soon as he got his, er, affairs in order. Ellen was patient, but never let up on the string of letters and phone calls reminding Jack of their magnificent destiny together. She performed many spiritual processes that were designed to clear his mind and bring him around to her way—that is, God's way—of thinking.

MORE BAD NEWS

One day, Barbara and I were talking to an acquaintance of both Ellen's and Jack's. He mentioned that Jack had indeed left Linda, but had married another woman, Karrie, just the previous evening. We knew Ellen and Jack had had breakfast together that very morning, so we wondered if he had mentioned this tidbit of information to his "intended." Apparently not. When we saw Ellen that afternoon, we had to break the news to her.

When Ellen heard that Jack had gotten married, her face drained of all color, but she recovered quickly. She just *knew* Jack would come around soon. After all, God had told her he was hers. She declared that it was such a high calling to win Jack, she would even humiliate herself to do it.

And humiliate herself she did. She started a letter-writing campaign to Jack's new wife, telling Karrie she was holding up God's plan and needed to step aside so the will of the Lord could go forth. Her harassment eventually broke up the marriage. (Maybe the fact that Karrie realized she was married to a lying, two-timing jerk helped.)

Ellen was jubilant when Jack left Karrie, but her joy was short-lived. Jack seemed to be avoiding her. Her calls weren't picked up, her long voicemails weren't returned, and her lengthy letters detailing her plans to improve Jack's spiritual fortitude went unanswered. (Could it possibly be that his standoffishness had something to do with Ellen running out of money to contribute to his ventures? Nah.)

Then came devastating news. Jack had moved back in with his original girlfriend, Linda. But all was not lost! Ellen was sure that with enough persuasion, and just one more spiritual clearing, Jack would see the light. The last we heard, she was still working feverishly to win him back. It goes without saying that her financial "investment" in the business end of the relationship has never returned a penny.

Even though it was obvious to any objective observer that Jack was not who he portrayed himself to be, Ellen just would not accept the evidence, nor would she question her defining belief about herself as a spiritually-advanced person who had a great destiny with this supposedly powerful and wealthy man. The walls she had built around her beliefs could not be breached by the most piercing salvos of information.

The problem Ellen had, and that we all can have when we build a Box, is that the world we create inside that Box defines us; it *is* us. Giving up our beliefs about ourselves may feel like a type of death. We may even feel as though we'll *actually* die if we allow our beliefs to collapse. Constant resistance to the reality outside our Box sometimes even leads to insanity, an example of which we'll give in a later chapter.

BELIEFS ARE APPROXIMATIONS
The key to maintaining your equilibrium, and even your reason, in the face of contradictions to your beliefs is to understand that your beliefs are not *you,* and they are never a finished product. The definition of a belief is that it is an *assumption* that something is true. So it is a *construction of your mind.* Beliefs are formed by information you are given that may or may not be correct. It is important to remember that a belief is always a rough calculation, not infallible TRUTH.

Beliefs Box You In

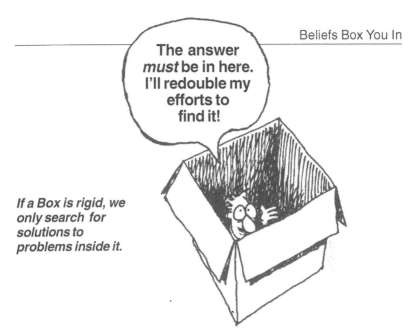

If a Box is rigid, we only search for solutions to problems inside it.

When we create *absolute* belief structures, such as those we are given with infallible religious dogma, inflexible family traditions, or even "proven" formulas for financial success, we fight any contradictions that appear. I find it heartbreaking to watch people become more and more rigid as they frantically manipulate their world to match their defining beliefs. They are in a closed-feedback loop with no apparent way to get out.

Having unquestioned beliefs is like driving a car that you never service. The engine gives you the ability to travel, but when it starts to make funny noises, you keep the hood down and hope for the best—instead of investigating what's wrong and making the necessary repairs. An enormous amount of your life and safety depends on the function of something you never check.

THE *BUT IT SHOULD HAVE WORKED* BOX

This next story, about someone we'll call Shawn, illustrates again the need to examine our beliefs and the Boxes we build around them. Shawn's father was a top executive in a multinational company. He set the standard for the success Shawn aspired to. Shawn followed his father into corporate America, getting a business degree and MBA along the way. He was hired by a large corporation, and over the years worked his way into upper management, becoming nationally known in his field.

The Collapse of Belief

Shawn believed his future was secure. After all, his father had worked for the same corporation his entire life; why would his career not follow the same pattern? Shawn eventually accumulated over a million dollars of stock in the company and was highly respected for his expertise on the cutting edge of his industry. He had a healthy, happy family and saw no reason to question his belief in his safety and security.

Then disaster hit. Shawn's company was decimated by fierce competition and a changing market, and he was laid off after 25 years of exemplary work. The changing fortunes of the business even destroyed his stock nest egg. After several years of fruitless job searching, he not only was still unemployed, but was diagnosed with a serious form of cancer.

Shawn had built his Box's walls with the mortar of certainty and complacency. He hadn't felt it necessary to watch for signs of change in his environment. He had invested everything in his belief that all was well, and was blindsided by the upheaval in his life. Even Shawn's health problems were largely a result of lifestyle issues he had chosen to ignore.

Our beliefs control our perception, which dictates our decisions, and that in turn creates The Box. The future we are all heading into is demanding, as never before, an awareness of our beliefs and the Boxes we create around them.

Here's something to be aware of: When holes appear in the

walls of your box, and you start to recognize that a belief may be crumbling, keep in mind that you may not have to change anything right away; just becoming aware of a flawed belief has an almost miraculous way of generating solutions to difficulties that were caused by it.

Being open to a resolution outside your belief system is the first step to allowing real transformation to occur in your life. This is what Einstein alluded to when he said that problems can never be solved on the same level on which they are created.

SOME BOXES ARE BENEFICIAL TO SOCIETY

It's important to remember that certain Boxes *should* remain solid. Some of the greatest achievements in history resulted from strong Boxes that stood up to punishing assaults.

Winston Churchill's Box was built on the belief that his country should never, never, never give in to the Nazis. George Washington resisted enormous pressure to accept the role of king offered to him after the Revolutionary War. His belief in freedom and democracy was too strong to allow him to succumb to the temptation of personal power and glory. Steve Jobs built a Box around his belief in his destiny to change the world of computers, then he relentlessly drove everyone in his company to fulfill that powerful dream.

A NEW KIND OF TOMORROW

We are headed into a future that will be different than any in recorded history. It will be more dynamic and unique than we can even imagine. Scientific knowledge is doubling every few years; global population is experiencing incredible growth; climate changes may alter the way we live; political systems around the world are embroiled in violent revolutions. All these conditions are converging to create dramatic transformations in life as we know it. It is imperative that we learn to distinguish between Boxes that should stand and those that need to be dismantled.

Our relationships keep us bound to our beliefs inside The Box.

4
Ties That Blind

The principal reason you stay locked in your Box of Belief is the confirmation you receive from others. That is why relationships are the prime factor that keeps you tied to your point of view. In other words, beliefs and relationships are inseparably intertwined; they hold each other in place.

If your beliefs collapse, your relationships will often collapse too. If you change your relationships first, it is almost inevitable that certain beliefs will change along the way. A lot of the pain that comes with the collapse of a belief can be traced to the loss of the relationships that were built on those beliefs.

Since your relationships validate your beliefs, relationships reinforce The Box, binding you together inside its walls. The disconnection of an important relationship can be a huge contradiction to your defining beliefs. Therefore, you cling to your relationships ferociously in order to confirm your beliefs. And you hold tight to your beliefs in order to maintain your relationships.

THE *BEING IMPORTANT* BOX,
OR HOW I INADVERTENTLY STARTED A CHURCH

Years ago I began to question the foundational precepts of the Mormon Church, of which I was then a member, and to seriously research its authentic history. During my investigation I

The Collapse of Belief

Jim's stack of copies of early Mormon history was almost as tall as he was.

heard rumors of a man in Ogden, Utah—a Realtor named Jim Harmston—who apparently had a boatload of documents that shed light on how early Mormon doctrine had been created. I was very interested in meeting him.

This was in the early 1990s, before the Internet, so copies of historical documents were hard to come by. There were whispers that Harmston even had in his possession little-seen documents that had been spirited out of LDS Church-owned university libraries—papers that dealt with the original revelations on such doctrines as priesthood, Church government and polygamy. When I tracked Jim down, I was astonished to find that the stack of Church-related papers he had was as tall as a man. He seemed to revel in being the owner of such rare and secret information, and would eagerly show them to people, making voluminous copies to distribute.

I became friends with Jim because of our mutual interest in Church history, and I subsequently taught him how to create visual models that would disseminate his knowledge in a compelling and easily-understood way. *(You can read more about my visual models in Chapter 10.)*

Jim caught on to the model-creating process quickly and began sharing his insights into church history and doctrine in this new, visual way. Many people were fascinated with the models, and Jim seemed to bask in the attention. He began to give sermons and to collect a following. I watched as Jim gathered more and more fans into his Box. His teachings began to become increasingly fundamentalist as he studied early church doctrines and tutored his enamored followers about the End of the World that was soon to come.

All this fundamentalism eventually led Jim and his wife, Elaine, to move to the rural town of Manti, Utah, where many Mormons of like mind were gathering to prepare for the winding-up scenes of this earth. Jim eventually started teaching his devotees that, in order to be in alignment with the original Mormon prophets' teachings, one must practice polygamy. He also lured followers into his Box by saying that they could get closer to God because of their association with him. In fact, Jim began to preach that he, himself, was Jesus Christ incarnate. (Gee, and I knew him when he was a mere Realtor.)

The same research that turned Jim into a religious fanatic led me out of the Mormon church. I visited Jim and Elaine a few times in Manti, and could see the direction they were heading, so I left and never saw them again. But I heard from friends that Jim formed his own church, which is still in existence today.

Jim strokes the egos of his admirers by telling them how important they were in a prior life and that they have a great destiny in this life. Being with Jim reinforces those beliefs about themselves. To lose the relationship would damage the belief, and vice versa.

Jim's disciples are even willing to give him large amounts of money and engage in illegal and debasing marital arrangements to maintain the relationship that validates their beliefs about themselves. Jim's belief about himself as a prophet and great leader is also dependent on his followers' adoration and approval.

One of the most tragic things, to me, about the story of Jim Harmston, has to do with his wife, Elaine. One day, before Jim had started his church, I was sitting in Elaine's kitchen, chatting with just her. I noticed a stack of snapshots lying on the table. Some of the pictures were of a beautiful, slim woman who looked like a model. When I asked who the woman was, Elaine said, "That's me, two years ago. " I was shocked because the Elaine standing before me was a very heavy woman who didn't resemble the lady in the photograph at all.

My Belief Window antennae started to poke up and I got curious about something. It had come up in some of our previous conversations that Elaine had had an affair a couple of years previously. So I asked her a question: "Elaine, was God involved in your affair?"

She looked stunned for a second; then said, "Yes, *damn him*, yes!" I said, "Why don't you ask God why it happened and what you're supposed to do?"

The Collapse of Belief

She began to cry, and eventually answered, "Because I'm afraid of what he might say."

Using hindsight, it seems that something (maybe her higher self?) was trying to pull Elaine out of a soon-to-be horrific scenario where she would end up as one of 21 wives. But Elaine's definition of herself was so invested in the role of being Jim's wife, she couldn't leave him.

The Box can stabilize us in dysfunction because of the interactions we engage in with others. Jim was able to manipulate Elaine and many others to agree with his view of the world, and since they wanted to maintain the connection (and keep their supposed link to God), they had to acquiesce to his way of thinking.

I have not seen Jim Harmston since he left the Mormon Church and started his own religion, but I have friends who have kept me up to date on his shenanigans. When people asked Jim how he learned to present his doctrines and prophecies in such an intriguing, visual way, he said angels had taught him. Now, I've been called a lot of things in my life, but never angelic!

When I was asked what I thought of Jim's massaging his personal history in that way, I decided a picture is worth a thousand words, so to answer, I did the drawing below.

When I taught Jim the model-making process, I inadvertently handed him a powerful tool to express his beliefs about himself. His desire to be a star drove him to seek more and more notoriety. He went from being an expert on church history, to a sought-after teacher, to a prophet with multiple wives, to God himself. But he was always expressing the same core belief. It just became more and more grotesque because he never stepped back and questioned his belief-creating or belief-expressing process. In all the time I knew Jim, I never once saw him look at himself objectively.

THE *MANAGER AS MONARCH* BOX

Barbara was once an executive in an international business. The C.O.O. of the company, Joe, demanded total submissiveness from all his employees. If someone ever hinted, by disagreeing with him in any way, or even an eye roll, that Joe didn't do everything perfectly, that person was fired immediately. Because of Joe's low self-esteem, and the way he compensated for it, he created an atmosphere of fear and insecurity throughout the company. Everyone had to be inside Joe's Box, validating his every move, or risk losing their job.

The sales manager, Walt, learned to play Joe's game well. He made it a point to pal around with Joe, agreeing with his take on things and even backing up his decisions to sack a continuous stream of people for supposed misdeeds. The only trouble was that Walt had a kind heart, so watching and even participating in Joe's horrendous management style began to take a toll on him. Walt started experiencing serious bouts of an inexplicable illness that put him in bed for weeks at a time.

After a couple of stressful years being Joe's lackey, Walt had finally had enough. He began the process of climbing out of Joe's Box. It wasn't easy because the walls had scary things written on them, such as, *You make a lot of money here—what are you thinking?* and, *What if you can't find another job?*

It was a struggle for Walt to get away from that company. And Joe did everything he could to keep him from leaving, including suing him for stealing trade secrets (as if common marketing techniques are somehow classified). Joe only wanted people to leave the company if he kicked them out; it was the ultimate invalidation if someone left because they couldn't stand him.

Barbara was proud of Walt for letting go of the belief that his only professional option was to stay with that company. He had to work hard to break free of the Box he and Joe were in, but he finally did it.

THE *PRINCESS* BOX

Sometimes people make a conscious decision to stay in a Box. The cost of leaving may be perceived as too high. Lori had a Box built around her Belief Window that said *I Am a Princess, and Everyone Must Serve Me.* All the people in her world had to be secondary to her and her wishes, or she would make their lives miserable.

Lori's husband Justin didn't decipher her Belief Window before he married her. Therefore, he found himself inside her Box as a court attendant. He was always running around serving her because that is the only way she would tolerate things.

If Justin had paid attention to Lori's mom's behavior before the wedding, he would have seen the same Belief Window. Princess Lori had been taught well by the Queen Mother.

One day Justin was at his wits' end, and he had a talk with his father-in-law, Frank, who served his own wife's every whim. Frank said: "I gave up fighting this situation years ago—the hell was just too much if I didn't knuckle under. I want to keep the family together, so I just do whatever my wife says. And if you want to keep *your* family together, you'd better do the same."

Frank knew on some level he was inside his wife's Box, dancing to her tune. It was draining and totally unfair, but he chose to stay, believing he had no other choice. Justin decided he didn't want to pay the price of his wife's displeasure, so he followed

The belief about the princess's superior position trumped everyone else's beliefs about themselves.

his father-in-law's example. To maintain the relationship he had to go blind to any alternative.

Was there a way out of those Boxes without breaking up the families involved? Maybe, but neither Justin nor Frank wanted to risk finding out what it was.

WAITING FOR MY ~~SHIP~~ AIRPLANE TO COME IN BOX

The next story is about a man we'll call Grant who was deep in a Box with a group of businessmen in southern California. He was assured that he would have access to an overseas insurance trust worth hundreds of millions of dollars if he would invest some money (substantial, of course) into making the deal go through. He wholeheartedly believed the transaction was legitimate, and pulled many of his family and friends into that Box to supply even more revenue—to the tune of millions of dollars.

Grant talked constantly about the imminent arrival of this huge amount of money and what he was going to do with it: the people he would help, the businesses he would start, and so on. His associates in California told him the cash would come in a private jet to the airport in his small town in Arizona. They gave him date after date, and he went to the airport faithfully to await the plane. Each time, there was an excuse why the jet didn't show up. Each time, they said they needed more money to finalize the deal.

Grant dutifully paid them and eagerly looked forward to his compensation. I was stunned when I found he had been doing this regularly for 14 years! The last I heard, he is still going to the airport to wait for the executive jet that will vindicate him. One of his sons said to me: "I don't think my father can do anything else but wait for the money to come in. He's invested too much of himself to admit he was wrong."

All Grant's friends left his Box when it became obvious the promised benefits weren't going to materialize. His family was the last to go, but they eventually climbed out. Grant is now alone inside his Box of Delusion peering through his Belief Window at the airport runway.

A POSITIVE BOX
Occasionally, a box can work to everyone's advantage. Here's a story that will warm your heart:

The Collapse of Belief

Margie was kind of a lost soul, wandering from job to job, and from school to school trying to figure out who she was. But Margie had an interesting Belief Window. It said *I See Good in Everyone*. When she met Greg, who was also pretty lost, she pulled him into her Box—where he began to believe in himself, and in her.

Margie and Greg eventually fell in love and got married. As they went through life, they worked together as a single high-functioning entity. It seemed to take the two of them to make one fully-capable person. Their synergy amazed everyone around them.

One crotchety old relative grudgingly admitted how well their relationship worked. He did say, however, "Those two wouldn't have amounted to anything without each other."

ORGANIZATIONAL BOXES

The relationship that groups have with their members in effect glues them together in a symbiotic Box. A church may keep its members inside its Box by promising eternal blessings in exchange for obedience and financial contributions. A company binds its employees to corporate procedures and responsibilities in return for a paycheck. These large Boxes are reinforced by the personal relationships taking place inside them that also confirm their rules and beliefs.

So, people often collude with each other in their group exchanges inside an organization to validate their shared beliefs and assure themselves they are right. It is rare to find a member of a cohesive group who is willing to challenge the status quo.

Barbara and I recently visited a museum in Germany dedicated to the resistance movement during World War II. One of the themes of the exhibits was that very few Germans stood up to the Nazis or worked to undermine Hitler's regime. The museum curator admitted this fact with sadness and chagrin.

The Enron Corporation is a classic example of a group Box in which everyone validated the prevailing wisdom (and benefited by it). As the Enron executives engaged in deceptive accounting practices that hid losses and exaggerated assets, almost everyone looked the other way. As the stock price shot up, and huge bonuses were awarded on anticipated future profits, virtually no one in the company questioned the corrupt system.

As is the case with many Boxes, where those in authority know the real story but perpetuate myths to keep their underlings compliant and in line, the leadership of Enron assured their employees that the company's positive financial projections were accurate. While they encouraged all stakeholders to keep their retirement funds invested in the company even when the price began to drop, the bosses were furiously unloading their stock. Some of them walked away with tens of millions of dollars.

As the stock price plunged from $90 a share to pennies, many employees who had planned to retire on their Enron stock saw their portfolios drop in value from nearly half a million to a few hundred dollars. After the corporation declared bankruptcy and was investigated by the government, several of the top company officials went to jail. One committed suicide, and the CEO was set to receive a prison term of 45 years, but died of a heart attack before sentencing. Enron's accounting firm, Arthur Anderson, was also a casualty of the collapse, folding because of unethical bookkeeping for its client.

The collective perception of Enron's employees had fueled its meteoric rise in the financial world. When the company Box finally imploded under the weight of its own dishonesty, the collapse was devastating for everyone involved.

5
Locking The Box Shut

People who are absolutely certain their beliefs are true have a tendency to lock their Box shut so no conflicting information can get in. They become susceptible to confirmation bias—paying attention only to evidence that confirms their beliefs. Then, in order to maintain their certainty amidst the contradictions that will inevitably come, they must manipulate information and situations to validate their correctness.

Securely locked Boxes will *always* attract opposition—it's just the nature of the beast, especially during times of change and upheaval. And that opposition can generate a split in the Box owners: A part of them promotes the correctness of their beliefs while the other part orchestrates a theatrical production to deflect attention away from the information they don't want to acknowledge. They create, in essence, a basement below their Box, full of stuff they don't want anyone to see. They may not even be aware of their stage-managing tactics.

In order to continue shielding themselves from inconvenient facts, people who are totally invested in certainty sink deeper and deeper into denial and duplicity, projecting the parts of their psyche they don't want to face onto others. They not only attempt to deceive those around them; they deceive themselves. And they collude with people of like mind, who are also in denial, to maintain the fantasyland of their perceived reality.

The Collapse of Belief

When we refuse to let go of our map of life even when the terrain changes—in other words, to avoid facing reality—we must create a world full of games and deception. A world in which we are constantly confirming our defining beliefs by enacting validating performances.

A classic example of this type of obfuscation is the administration of President George W. Bush during the Iraq War. Even after it became obvious that the invasion was a fiasco resulting from erroneous reports of weapons of mass destruction, the Bush PR machine vehemently justified the war, which cost thousands of American lives and almost a trillion dollars, along with the deaths of hundreds of thousands of Iraqis.

To this day, interviewers cannot get Bush or former vice president Dick Cheney to admit they made a mistake in their pre-emptive attack on a country that has never directly threatened the United States.

The main activity of someone locked in their Box is to make sure others accept and confirm their beliefs. This requires a relentless production of validating stories, as Bush and Cheney demonstrate.

THE REDECORATED BOX

Sometimes, when we are hit with a contradiction we can't deny, we are able to scramble around and repackage our beliefs into a different configuration inside our Box. This is easier than facing and dismantling an erroneous defining belief—especially one hidden deep in the basement of our Box that we are not fully aware of. When we can hold onto some vestiges of a defining belief that has worked for us, we would rather modify it than allow it to completely collapse, and start over.

Lorraine had a Belief Window she was not consciously aware of that said *I Am Superior.* She expressed that belief in many ways. She divorced her husband because he wasn't righteous enough and as diligent in his religious duties as she. Her superiority also manifested itself in her pride in being a devout fundamentalist Christian. She felt better than her non-fundamentalist neighbors because of her membership in God's One True Church.

But a perplexing chain of events led Lorraine to the conclusion that the leaders of her religion were dishonest and manipulative. She was devastated, and decided to leave her church. She subsequently joined a mainstream Protestant denomination, from which she continued to look down upon non-Christians.

Lorraine liked her new church because its rules were less strict than her old religion. But she wasn't willing to let go of her hidden defining belief. She simply orchestrated a new manifestation of her superiority.

THE BASEMENT OF AN ORGANIZATION'S BOX

Way down in the cellar of almost any organization's Box is the belief that the system must survive at all costs. That belief drives behavior more than any promoted ideal. The quality or quantity of work the entity does is secondary to its continued existence. But that hidden belief is never acknowledged, at least publicly.

I became aware of the true governing belief of a certain school system's Box one day when I had a private conversation with a top state school administrator. I was talking with him about implementing a curriculum that would break down the barriers between subjects, creating a more holistic learning environment. The official closed his office door and said to me, "I'm going to tell you something that I will deny if you ever say I said it." He then explained that he was retiring in two weeks, so he would be very frank.

"The educational system has no interest in any meaningful improvement," he said. "It is only concerned with its institutional survival, and it will always put more energy into that objective than any other."

The official went on to tell me that even though the system promotes innovation, it is more concerned with its preservation, and reforms that threaten the status quo would always be sabotaged. He mentioned dozens of excellent programs he had personally reviewed that were never implemented. "Even though the school system touts quality education," he said, "the real priority is maintaining power." He was not proud of this state of affairs but had no ability to change it. He then opened his office door and ushered me out.

Of course, the public declarations of any system will loudly proclaim its focus on the professed objectives of the organization, but here's a tool to help you see if something is fishy: The number-one indication that something duplicitous is going on *is the effort to stop you from seeing.* If you are warned against looking at material that opposes the tenets to which an organization adheres, your critical-thinking buzzers should go off.

The rules for organizations are true for people also. Not only do we do mental gymnastics to maintain our own convictions, we perform elaborate contortions to convince others that what we believe is true. And the more disharmony there is between the environment outside the Box and the belief inside, the more involved the distortions must become.

It's kind of like having a map of Disneyland, but you're standing in Minnesota in the winter. If you sincerely believe your map is accurate, you will tell yourself (and others) all sorts of things to make sense of the terrain—even as your feet freeze.

Unfortunately, almost everyone is guilty of this type of duplicity at one time or another. We pound our environment into matching our beliefs instead of adapting to the reality that's usually right in front of our faces. Because of self-deception, and a certain amount of laziness, we pay attention to only what we want to see. But when dishonesty and dysfunction become extreme, things blow up. That's when we have the opportunity to question our own beliefs, *and* the emphatic assertions of others.

THE LOCKED *I WANT MY WAY* BOX

I once knew a man I'll call Harold who was in a property dispute with a woman with whom he was negotiating a real estate deal. As the bargaining got more and more acrimonious, Harold got so mad he deliberately ran into her car with his bulldozer.

The woman filed assault charges, but Harold denied he had done it. Harold's business partner believed him. He accepted the belief on Harold's Window that said *I Am an Honest and Reasonable Man*. The partner got inside Harold's Box and went to great lengths to support Harold through the court proceedings. He couldn't imagine that his partner would be that aggressive or violent. He didn't want to consider that Harold may have a hidden belief in his Box's basement that said *I Am Justified in Doing Whatever it Takes to Get My Way.*

At the court deposition, a videotape of the incident, taken by a bystander, appeared. There on the screen was Harold yelling at the woman, threatening to run her down if she didn't yield to his demands. It then showed him ramming his tractor into her car.

Harold's partner was stunned. He said later, "I believed Harold right up until I saw the tape." He subsequently paid the woman a settlement and severed all business ties with Harold. He was finally willing to let his belief in his partner collapse, but it took seeing indisputable evidence of Harold's deceit.

SEEING INTO A FATHER'S HEART

I know a man who hired his son to work for his company. I was also associated with the business and watched the interactions between father and son. One day the son came up with a good idea to increase sales in a selected area. You'd think a father would be proud of his son's innovation, and support it. What I saw was that the father's need to be superior to his son and prove him wrong was stronger than whatever love he had.

The dad deliberately sabotaged the implementation of his son's idea by giving misleading information to suppliers, withholding sufficient funds to make the plan work, and diverting necessary staff to other projects.

As I watched the situation, I could see this man's governing beliefs emerge from the basement of his Box. I realized his obsession to be right and better than everyone else would also undermine me in the long run. Armed with this discernment, I made the decision to never be involved in business with that person again.

O.J.'S BOX

When we build a Box around our beliefs to protect our definitions of ourselves and our world—then lock it down with our certainty—the violent defense of the image we hold up for everyone to see can turn truly ugly.

Before O.J. Simpson was charged with murder, the world thought of him as a superb athlete, a rich and famous actor, and an all-around great guy. When his ex-wife Nicole threatened that image by rejecting him and therefore challenging his definition of himself, he had to destroy the contradiction—killing her along with her friend Ron Goldman, who was also part of the dissonance.

The tragic thing about denying ourselves the opportunity to question our defining beliefs is that when we bury contradictions, the pressure builds up until it explodes into something much worse than the original problem. If O.J. had simply been able to look at

The Collapse of Belief

himself honestly, his issues would probably never have escalated into murder.

Simpson's acquittal at his trial allowed him to dive deep into denial, only to have the issue seep out and express itself in a robbery incident a few years later, for which he was convicted and sent to jail. I'll go out on a limb here and make a prediction: O.J.'s temper will resurface in prison. It's easy to see this coming because there are certain questions he is refusing to ask. He doesn't want to face even the smallest contradiction about himself. His Box is locked tight.

One of the deepest of human fears is that we are not what we believe ourselves to be. And in order to avoid facing the truth, we orchestrate events and interactions, then deny—even to ourselves—that we are manipulating anything. This entire process is an act of creation: first we create a belief that defines us, then we create the confirming stories and scripts we follow, which creates the Box we then inhabit.

Underneath all this creating is a deep problem: The playacting we all engage in is the automatic reaction to our fear of exposure. it is simply too painful to allow anyone to see that we are not who we purport to be, or to admit that what we champion as fact doesn't completely hold water. This behavior is endemic to society and is probably the major dysfunction of the civilized world.

Locking The Box Shut

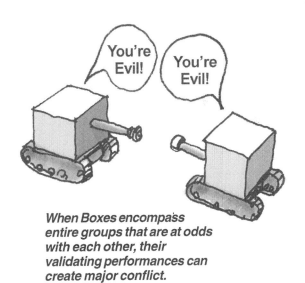

When Boxes encompass entire groups that are at odds with each other, their validating performances can create major conflict.

Society is full of Boxes whose occupants are determined to stay inside--even as they crumble.

Some brave souls accept the collapse and allow for new options.

6
When the Box Collapses

There are two ways to handle a collapse of belief:

1. *Accept the collapse and move toward the new paradigm in which you find yourself, or*
2. *Resist the change and hunker down in a state of denial, relentlessly imposing your delusional world on not only yourself, but those around you.*

In any serious collapse there is always some kind of death: financial, social, spiritual, relational or even physical, so your survival instinct kicks in as your world falls apart. Your first reaction is usually to circle the wagons and protect yourself from the unwanted information or disastrous situation.

Because we have a tendency to make beliefs real, we confuse our defining beliefs with ourselves, and their loss feels as though we ourselves are dying.

One of the hardest periods of my life was when the foundational beliefs with which I defined myself collapsed. At one particular time I was in such pain and fear, I found myself in agony, curled up in a fetal position on the bathroom floor. I felt as if I were dying, and I was actually surprised later to find myself still alive.

Following are stories about a few people who experienced a

severe collapse of their world view. Some of them found the gold in their circumstances and created something positive out of the rubble, and others refused to accept the new reality being foisted upon them, descending into near or outright insanity.

RE-CREATING A FUTURE
We mentioned Tamara in Chapter 1. She and her husband were working hard so they could retire in style. They had everything mapped out: where they would live, what they would do, etc. When he died suddenly of a heart attack in his mid forties, Tamara's world collapsed. Her whole definition of herself changed. Who was she without her partner? What would she do with the rest of her life?

Tamara had to rebuild her life; she had little choice. She decided to go massage school, where she discovered a rare talent for energy work. Tamara has since changed many people's lives with her gift. Her career has opened up a whole new world of wonder and fulfillment. She says: "I sometimes find myself thanking my husband for dying. Without his death, I would never have become who I am today."

AN UNBENDING BELIEF
There is a sad story in Mormon history that is little-known even to its members. It's the story of David Hyrum Smith, the youngest son of LDS Church founder Joseph Smith. David was born four months after his father was killed in Carthage, Illinois.

David's mother, Emma Hale Smith, wanted to preserve the reputation of her husband as a noble man and a true prophet. After his murder, most of the church members went west to

Utah with Brigham Young, but Emma stayed in Illinois to raise her family. She understandably abhorred the principle of plural marriage (polygamy) that Brigham had secretly learned under Joseph's tutelage, and she did not want her children tainted with the practice.

Emma categorically denied that her husband had ever been married to anyone but her, and she taught her children to honor and respect their father as a virtuous man and a key mouthpiece for God. David grew up with the unshakable belief that his father had been a great religious leader whose morals were above reproach—a belief that gave him a sense of his place in the world.

As an adult, however, David traveled to Utah and came up against irrefutable proof that his father had not only instigated the practice of polygamy, but had engaged in it in quite problematic ways——marrying underage girls and wooing married women away from their husbands. In Utah, he met his half-siblings and women who swore in affidavits they had wedded his father while simultaneously being married to someone else.

The contradiction was too much for David. He could not reconcile the facts in front of him with his absolute belief in his parents' integrity. *It could not be true that his father had used religion as a cover for his sexual proclivities! It was impossible that his beloved mother had lied to him so profoundly!*

David never could restructure his beliefs to allow for reality, and he eventually went insane. He spent the last 20 years of his life in a mental institution. He simply would not let his beliefs about his family and his personal worldview collapse.

AN ATHEIST'S COLLAPSE OF BELIEF
The late Christopher Hitchens was a famous nonbeliever in religion and a promoter of social change around the globe. He wrote countless articles and many books arguing his take on world events. In one magazine article, back in 1979, Hitchens praised the agenda of the up-and-coming leader of Iraq, Saddam Hussein. Later, when it became evident Hussein was not the benevolent president he purported himself to be, Hitchens changed his beliefs about the dictator and retracted his statements, even working to expose Hussein's atrocities against the Iraqi people.

The Collapse of Belief

In describing his turnaround, Hitchens quoted the axiom, "When facts change, opinions must change." He was willing to let go of his convictions even though he had declared them publicly and vehemently. Whether or not you agree with Hitchens' political or religious views, it's hard not to admire his integrity.

WHEN THE ONLY SOLUTION TO A CONTRADICTION IS DEATH

History is littered with examples of religious cult members who would rather die than face a glaring contradiction to their faith. They can't allow for the possibility that their revered leader may have the makings of a psychotic megalomaniac, or even be slightly off-kilter.

The followers of Jim Jones and the People's Temple in Guyana are an example of carrying an absolute belief in an authority figure to the ultimate extreme. Nine hundred people were willing to ingest cyanide-laced soft drinks, and sacrifice their lives as well as those of their family, rather than seriously examine the doctrines they were being taught, or their leader's motives. Their stubborn refusal to look outside their devoutly-constructed Box resulted in the iconic warning to the world that has become synonymous with accepting information uncritically: "Don't drink the Kool-Aid."

A HUSBAND'S STORY

Tim had a temper problem, but he would never admit it. His wife Stacie despaired of getting him to face the issue and deal with it. Since he adamantly refused to acknowledge his culpability in any of their marriage problems, Stacie reluctantly divorced him, feeling as though she had no other option.

Well, Tim was furious with his wife for kicking him out, but he still couldn't see that any of their problems were his fault. *If she could just understand how irritating her behavior is*, he thought.

One day Tim was talking with a counselor to figure out how to get on with his life after the breakup. The therapist suggested that he could not go forward until he learned to manage his anger. Hearing someone besides his wife bring up this issue brought Tim up short. He decided that maybe there was something to what his wife had complained about, after all. Tim swallowed his pride and apologized to his ex-wife and worked diligently on overcoming the dysfunction he had previously energetically denied. *(Note: Tim unconsciously made use of a perspective tool we will elaborate more on in Chapter 7.)*

A WIFE'S STORY
Cheryl is a mother of six children who had quite severe lower back pain for years. She decided the best way to cope with it was to stay in bed, so she became a semi-invalid at age 42. Her husband worked full-time and also took care of everything in the household: cooking, cleaning, shopping, parenting, and tenderly nursing Cheryl. He had a cheerful attitude and never complained. After all, his wife was crippled.

One morning, Cheryl reached over to pat her husband in bed, and found him cold and still. He had passed away of a brain aneurism in the night with no warning. After the funeral, Cheryl found herself in a quandary. Who would take care of her and the children? No one seemed to be available. The only thing to do was to get up and do it herself. And guess what? She found ways to cope with her pain, and even discovered treatments to nearly eliminate it.

Cheryl raised her children with her husband's life insurance settlement and began working full-time in a satisfying profession. One day she said to a friend: "I sometimes wonder if God took my husband to teach me a lesson."

NEVER PICTURING THAT FUTURE
Sometimes a person or organization is looking ahead for changes that might occur, but still neglects to take advantage of information that appears. The Eastman Kodak Company is a poignant example. Even though 30 years ago Kodak developed some of the first digital camera technology, they were reluctant to phase out their celluloid film manufacturing that had been their bread and butter for nearly a century.

Because the company executives couldn't let go of their belief that their analog product would always be in demand, they lagged behind all the other innovators in the market. At this writing, Kodak has just filed for bankruptcy, bringing to an effective end a company that once dominated its industry.

A TALE OF TWO CHURCHES
The Mormon (LDS) Church has numerous offshoots, only a few of which have survived over the nearly two centuries of the

religion's existence. Two of the splinter groups have an interesting history, mainly because of the differing ways they have handled contradictions to their doctrine and traditions.

One of the sects is the Reorganized Church of Jesus Christ of Latter-day Saints (RLDS), founded by a son of Joseph Smith after the main body of the church went west. The other is the Fundamentalist Church of Jesus Christ of Latter-Day Saints (FLDS), which was formed in Utah to continue the practice of polygamy after it was disavowed by the LDS prophet in 1890.

These two groups are a study in contrast. When serious questions began to arise more than 20 years ago about the authenticity of the Book of Mormon as a bona-fide historical record, the RLDS Church studied the evidence and allowed for the possibility that this book of scripture might be a mythological story fabricated by 19th century religionists. As a result of that ambiguity, RLDS leaders have granted their members the option to believe whether or not the book is divinely inspired. In interviews with RLDS Church officials, it is clear they knew this admission would negatively impact their membership numbers, but they felt it was the most integrous way to go.

True to projections, a huge number of people left the RLDS Church in the wake of this acknowledgment. Membership rolls went from 250,000 to 40,000. The church also decided to discontinue what they saw as discrimination against women, and began ordaining females to the priesthood. That policy culled even more die-hard traditionalists from the ranks. In keeping with their new direction, the church changed its name to The Community of Christ.

Now for the FLDS Church. Their obsession to hang onto their beliefs at any price has cost their members dearly. Not only have they continued what some call the barbaric and degrading practice of plural marriage, they have steadfastly shielded their members from any information that would challenge their beliefs: The Internet is forbidden in members' homes; tapes of church leaders' sermons are required listening; and disobedience to the prophet results in ostracism and loss of family and property.

As this community becomes more and more isolated and insular in their beliefs, the behavior of their current prophet, Warren Jeffs, has become more and more bizarre. Even though he is serving a life prison sentence for sexual abuse, he continues to thrash his followers from jail with stricter and stranger edicts. The latest is the banning of all toys for children and all electronic gadgets, such as cell phones, for adults. He has declared every marriage null and void, effectively prohibiting sex until he can come back and re-marry everyone. Jeffs blames Church members for his incarceration: He tells them that if they were more righteous, the walls of the prison would fall down.

But the most chilling of Jeffs' pronouncements has to do with blood atonement. He is resurrecting a forgotten and renounced doctrine of Brigham Young that requires the shedding of one's blood for full repentance of certain sins. Those watching the FLDS society are worried about a mass suicide on the order of Jonestown.

So there you have examples of how two similar organizations dealt with contradiction: One with integrity, doing what it felt was the honest thing, even though it would cost the church in membership and financial contributions; the other with a fanatical obsession to maintain the status quo, steadfastly ignoring any and all indications that the group might be on the wrong path.

A CHOICE ABOUT ONE'S COLLAPSING BELIEF

When pilots are taught to fly airplanes, they are trained to trust their instruments—even when their senses are giving them contradictory input. A pilot's equilibrium may be skewed by the plane's position, and he may feel as though his plane is upside down when it is not. A pilot who doesn't pay attention to the facts his instrument panel is telling him, and relies instead on his feelings, could fly his plane right into a mountain. In the same way, when we allow fear and insecurity, or even certainty, to rule us instead of seeking out and accepting objective facts, we may be courting disaster, not only for ourselves, but for all those journeying with us on our metaphorical airplane.

World traveler and Internet blogger Brandon Pearce described the struggle between one's feelings and the need to face reality when he said, "Emotion is the enemy of objectivity." When Pearce was facing a huge paradigm shift in his life, sentimentality for his old, comfortable ways nearly convinced him to abandon his search for truth. But in the end he realized that the rewards of being true to himself outweighed the ease of remaining in delusion. You can read his story at pearceonearth.com.

7
Conscious Believing

Human beings are meaning-makers. We have a deep need to make sense of the world, and we do that with beliefs. But beliefs aren't what you think they are; when you believe something, you assume you *know* it. But you really only *think* it. A belief isn't necessarily reality; it's a construction of your mind, built to give meaning, as we said in Chapters 2 and 3.

We create beliefs through metaphors—by equating something to something else. And we *need* beliefs; they are how we navigate through life. As Jonathan Haidt said in *The Happiness Hypothesis*: "Our life is the creation of our minds, and we do much of that creating in metaphor. With the wrong metaphor we are deluded; with no metaphor we are blind."

Using metaphors, we build maps, or models, in our minds that give us a paradigm in which to function. But it's important to realize that those maps are only approximations; they can never be absolutely true or real; they merely give you a way to operate with the information you have at the time.

Just as your brain makes an image of an object which the eye sees, the brain also makes a model of a situation which becomes a paradigm, or belief.

WHEN THE REPRESENTATION BECOMES REAL
The hazard we face when dealing with beliefs is in being unable to scrutinize them with detachment. We are too prone to accept without question the governing paradigms of our family, say, or a particular group to which we belong. We are conditioned from childhood to never question the underlying assumptions to which our culture adheres. But believing is an evolutionary and ever-changing process. If beliefs are not examined critically at some point, human progress would grind to a halt. Just consider all the goofy beliefs people have had down through time, from the sun orbiting the earth to bloodletting as a cure for disease. And look at things you used to believe that you now see as crazy.

THE MOST DOMINANT BELIEFS
Our most powerful beliefs are subliminal, and they can be the most dangerous. For instance, you may have this subconscious belief: *I should base my life on what someone else says is true.* Another one could be: *I'm not enough. A certain person (or organization) has something that will make me more.*

It's important to understand the difference between knowledge and belief. You can only *know* something that you have direct experience with: *I am here; That hurts; This chair is hard,* etc. Some things that you think you *know,* you really only *believe.* Even saying, "I know the sky is blue," isn't completely intellectually honest. It only *appears* to be blue from your vantage point.

To say, "I know that such-and-such is true," can only be accurate if you have first-hand knowledge of that concept or event. If you don't have direct experience with the phenomenon, you can *know* that it makes you feel a certain way, but you *believe* it is true.

One way we maintain our beliefs is by circular reasoning. Here's an example:

Heidi: "I'm positive Michael never lies."

Jane: "How do you know?"

Heidi: "Because he told me so."

Another example: *The Bible is true because it says right on its pages that it comes from God.*

Circular reasoning can also consist of an appeal to authority: *So-and-so said it, so it must be true.*

People in positions of power make beliefs out to be real in order to maintain control: Parents tell their children the bogeyman will get them if they don't behave; churches use belief to keep the faithful in line: *You'll go to hell if you don't do what we say.* These threats would have no clout if they weren't wholeheartedly believed.

Sometimes we keep the trappings of a belief even after the actual conviction fades away. It's like having a prettily-wrapped gift; we might keep the shiny box long after the present is no longer useful. An example of this could be the "lost boys" of the polygamous community in Colorado City, Arizona, who left the town because they no longer believed in that lifestyle, or were kicked out to reduce competition for young brides.

These boys let go of their belief that the FLDS prophet speaks for God, but they didn't know how to let go of the cultural "wrapping" that teaching came in. They had been programmed to follow orders and had never been trained to think for themselves. Many of them struggled to integrate into the self-determining outside society. They sank into drug and alcohol addiction, and substituted video games for real life in a desperate attempt to survive in an entirely new paradigm.

A CIRCLE OF VIEWPOINTS
One of the best ways to analyze your beliefs is to incorporate several viewpoints. Seeing a situation from multiple perspectives has a powerful way of expanding your view and changing your perception. I'll never forget the experience I had of walking into an empty art classroom one day when I was teaching at a university. The room was empty except for about a dozen easels set up in a circle. Each easel had a drawing pad on it with a completed portrait. The pads also had other markings on them: teacher's notes, food stains, and the like.

As I walked around the circle, looking at each drawing, an image began to emerge of what had been in the center of the room—a beautiful young woman. What had formerly been invisible began to appear. But I could only get a complete idea of what she looked like by studying *all* the pictures.

And I also saw more: I could tell what the students had been

The Collapse of Belief

eating while they drew, who the students were, who the model was, what kind of mood she was in, who the teacher was, what *his* mood had been, what they had all talked about, and why nobody was there.

Each easel was a point of view, and together they brought into my awareness what was formerly invisible. Every picture was different, but each was a window into what had happened, and was valid in its own way. Observing the different points of view created a complete image of the entire interaction in the classroom.

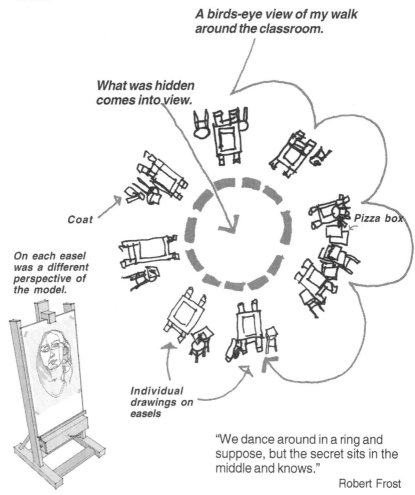

A birds-eye view of my walk around the classroom.

What was hidden comes into view.

Coat

On each easel was a different perspective of the model.

Pizza box

Individual drawings on easels

"We dance around in a ring and suppose, but the secret sits in the middle and knows."

Robert Frost

EACH ELEMENT GAVE A PIECE OF THE PUZZLE

The drawings, when taken together, acted as transparencies, each one overlapping and enhancing the others. I might look at a model's expression or body language and see boredom. You might see pensive. But when we take all twelve perspectives, each one relating to and thus enhancing the others, we are going to see a truer picture of the person and her mood.

The food stains tell you who was preoccupied: Who can slam pizza with one hand while drawing a portrait with another? The teacher's notes provide insight into what was discussed.

Who were the students? Why, just read the names in the corners of the drawing. What artist does not sign his or her work? At least a few of them have given their work the same name as the model, so we know who she was.

And where are they now? They're close. Not here, but somewhere nearby because class is still in session and they left personal belongings behind.

When we can see something from many perspectives, we begin to think differently, and what is unseen can come into sight. In reality, there is no such thing as a single point of view. There *are* systems and organizations, however, that insist there is just one way to see things–their way. But it is only by dancing the dance through multiple perspectives that the real truth appears.

I can see why certain groups sometimes pound so hard on one viewpoint: As soon as people start seeing multiple perspectives, an organization cannot maintain the narrow perception it wants its members to have.

THINKING HOLISTICALLY

As you strive to think more holistically, you must respect each individual viewpoint. Every perspective is legitimate, and in fact necessary, to prevent tunnel vision. Observing something from only one viewpoint restricts your view. It's like walking around looking through a toilet paper tube, thinking you can see everything.

Just as I could see hidden aspects of that situation in the classroom only by looking at it from many angles, the more perspectives we can see in life, the more clearly we will be able to discern the truth. As conditions change around us, it is imperative that we construct new beliefs in response to information that presents itself in our environment. A crucial element for beneficial belief construction is accurate observation. And the most accurate observation comes from multiple viewpoints.

Once you learn to observe a situation from several perspectives you will begin to acquire discernment, which is characterized by keen insight and good judgment. You will be able to comprehend things that are obscure or even invisible to those around you.

If you only see one way,
you only think one way.
If you only think one way,
you can only respond one way.
If you only respond one way,
you cannot change.

Here's a hint to help you become a better observer: The clues to what you should see are usually right in front of your face; you just have to unhook from your usual way of looking. You must to be willing to take off your blinders, which consist of value judgments, biases, conditioning and opinions—and consider *all* the facts.

John Chafee describes this process elegantly in his book *Thinking Critically:*

> *We need to have the emotional willingness to open ourselves to new possibilities and the intellectual ability to see issues from different perspectives. Very often people are so emotionally entangled in their point of view that*

they are simply unwilling to question its truth, and so the power of their emotional needs inhibits the potential illumination of their reasoning abilities.

BELIEF INTEGRATION

A useful way to analyze a belief is to explore its opposite—because contained within *every* belief is its antithesis.

For example, the belief *I Have the Truth* also means *You Don't Have the Truth*. Or the belief *My Three College Degrees Make Me Important* also means *Your Lack of Education Means You're Less Valuable*. If someone believes *My Needs are the Most Vital,* then s/he also believes *Your Needs Don't Need to be Addressed.*

If you look at the complement to one of your defining beliefs, and see that it might not be 100 percent true, your belief might have holes in it.

You'll notice that the more absolute a belief is, the more extreme its counterpart becomes, which actually makes it easier to examine.

SUMMARY

Conscious believing means taking ownership of what you believe. That means understanding what a belief is: *a mental construction*; and what it isn't: *absolute truth* (which it never can be).

If you are in tremendous pain about a belief collapsing, you need to at least know what you're dealing with. Seeing multiple viewpoints can clarify your beliefs and expand your view of reality. You will be able to see more clearly how you built your beliefs in the first place.

So if a belief really is a construction, what is so terrible about its collapse? It's mainly the peripheral things around the belief that cause the trauma: the loss of your sense of meaning, your definition of yourself, damaged relationships with family and friends, etc. But if you can step outside your Box of Belief, set your Belief Window aside, and view beliefs as what they really are, the loss of a belief itself doesn't need to have such a devastating impact on your life.

A loudly-proclaimed belief does not necessarily drive behavior.

Observe actions to discern the real defining belief.

8
Redefining Your Defining Beliefs

Suppose you have a stomach ache. Do you think it's important to know whether the pain is coming from indigestion, or an ulcer? Of course it is. You need to know what you're dealing with before you can treat it effectively.

The same is true when you're experiencing the pain of a collapsing belief. The more accurately you can identify what you actually believe, the more effectively you can deal with your beliefs changing or collapsing. Sometimes we're fuzzy about what we really believe. If you can nail it down, you may find that there's an easier way to handle the trauma than you thought.

THE *I SHOULD STAY IN THIS MARRIAGE* BELIEF
Tom was in a marriage that he knew wasn't entirely healthy, but he loved his wife and believed that staying together was the best thing to do. When he discovered that his wife was having an affair, he was in anguish over the betrayal and the loss of his dream of the forever partnership. The only place he could go to have privacy in his home was a walk-in closet, so he spent hours there rocking in pain in the dark, coming to the realization that his wife's conduct had become more and more bizarre lately.

Then Tom calmed down and began to ask himself some questions: "Is this relationship really where I want to be?" and, "Is there any indication that my wife will ever face the childhood abuse that is probably causing her aberrant behavior?" When he realized that the answer to both questions was "no," Tom began to recognize that his belief about needing to stay in the marriage was faulty. He also saw that the deep depression he had been in for the previous several years had its roots in his dysfunctional relationship, and that the only thing that would save his health and sanity was to leave the marriage.

With this new understanding, the grief Tom felt about the dissolution of his marriage suddenly went away. He formed a new belief that said *Taking Care of Myself is More Important than Supporting a Sick Relationship*. He was surprised that along with this new belief came a mental clarity that gave him ideas about how to separate from his wife cleanly and fast. After his divorce he eventually married a woman with whom he formed a stable and happy union. Tom often reflects now that if he came across the man who seduced his wife, he would thank him.

THE *MY DAD IS BAD* BELIEF

Kyle had issues with his father. He thought he was unreasonable and controlling. His dad also had a sharp sense of humor that often wounded Kyle's feelings. Because he was the firstborn, the dynamic between Kyle and his dad was different than that between his four siblings and their father; they didn't seem to have the same type of association with him as he did.

As Kyle became an adult, his resentment of his father deepened and festered. During his training to become a psychologist he became convinced that all his problems and neuroses were the result of his parenting. Kyle felt justified in punishing his dad by cutting off communication and excluding him from family events. He also began to recruit his brothers and sisters to his way of thinking about their father. Since he could give scientific-sounding reasons for his behavior, he was very persuasive. When the siblings began to participate in persecuting Dad, it bolstered Kyle's belief about how right he was.

Kyle's father was bewildered and hurt by the way his children were suddenly treating him. When he attempted to question them, they were evasive and dismissive. Kyle had thoroughly convinced them that their dad was destructive and should be avoided at all costs.

Redefining Your Defining Beliefs

One son-in-law, however, was puzzled by the situation. He could see nothing in the dad's actions to warrant such treatment. One day he had a long talk with his wife, questioning her closely about her father. At first she talked in general terms about how dangerous her father was, then as her husband pressed for more details, she mumbled, "Well, Kyle says, uh, we need to do this."

The son-in-law was finally able to show his wife her real belief: *I Must Punish my Dad Because my Brother Says to, Not Because of Anything He Did to Me.* When she could see the absurdity of that belief, she dropped it, apologized to her dad, and reestablished a relationship with him.

So, seeing through incongruities lets you perceive your hidden beliefs. You can bring them upstairs into the light, so to speak, and deal with them out in the open. A useful tool is to restate the belief—saying in it a way that incorporates all the peripheral assumptions attached to the main belief. For example, a member of a strict religion who says, *I Believe in Free Agency* could qualify the belief with its peripheral assumption: *I am Only Free to Choose what my Church Leaders Say.* A child brought up with a sense of entitlement might believe *My Parents Should Serve Me.* The peripheral assumption is *I Owe my Parents Nothing*—or—*I am Not Committed to Equitable Exchanges.* A stingy employer's proclaimed belief that *I Always Take Care of My Workers* could be restated as *I Will Give Whatever Benefits the Law Compels Me To.*

SET ASIDE YOUR BELIEF WINDOW AND *LOOK*

Jean grew up with a father who was a pillar of the community. He held high positions in his church and was elected to important offices in local government. Jean created a Belief Window about him that said *My Father is a Great and Good Man.*

Years later, when Jean had children of her own, she discovered that her father had sexually molested her oldest daughter. Jean was shocked, but was not able to let go of her belief about him. As a consequence, she did not bring legal charges against him or even report him to his ecclesiastical authorities. Her inability to set aside her Belief Window and view the situation objectively prevented her from protecting her other children. Her father subsequently molested more of his granddaughters over the years.

Even into old age, Jean continued to view her father through her

The Collapse of Belief

Belief Window. She didn't recognize her hidden belief: *The Idealized Image of my Father is More Important than the Facts.* When she sang his praises around her children and kept a large photograph of him on her bedside table, her daughters felt continually abused, even long after their grandfather's death. It took years of counseling for them to understand their mother's hidden belief, and realize why she did the things she did.

The biggest block to accurately reading beliefs is the need to validate yourself.

A LITTLE SECRET

One of the most helpful things you can do to allow for new information about yourself is to detach from the need to validate your beliefs—those about yourself as well as the ones held by any group to which you belong. To practice, try this experiment: see if you can get through an entire conversation without validating yourself or your beliefs one time. Watch for phrases like, "This is the way I see it," or "I did this," or "I have the answer to your problem."

I practiced this for a long time (and I'm still working at it). The first time I got through an entire phone call without validating myself once I felt as though I deserved a medal. It sounds simple, but it's harder than you think!

Barbara and I have become deeply committed to this principle—

that our ability to see accurately is in direct proportion to our ability to corral the ego. We even had a plaque made up for our house that says, "The More Validation I Need, the Less Discernment I Have."

If you ever start to analyze your own central beliefs, you are stepping into new territory. Most likely, no one around you has ever gone where you're going. Few people ever question their fundamental beliefs or those of the systems they support—it doesn't even cross their minds to do so. So when your beliefs are changing, if you can free yourself from the need to use others to validate your process, by turning off the need to explain yourself or get them to agree with your position, you will have less conflict with people around you. You will never completely get rid of the tendency to validate yourself; no one does. Just learn to turn it off and on, kind of like a light switch.

A reciprocal cycle of belief validation can trap us in intractable relationships. When we constantly tell each other, and ourselves, that we're correct in our beliefs, we lock ourselves out of the probability of change and growth. And the more we invest in an unhealthy relationship, the less likely we are to shift.

This is one reason you won't see the political situation in Washington D.C. changing anytime soon. All the players in that arena mutually benefit by confirming each other's beliefs. They are all involved in a collusion of validation.

REDEFINING DEFINING BELIEFS

It is refreshing to see someone honestly evaluate their defining beliefs and make positive changes. Paul was one person who did so with courage and determination. Paul's wife had divorced him, which had imploded his world. Instead of nursing his wounds and becoming resentful, however, Paul asked himself a crucial question: "I wonder why she doesn't want to live with me." He looked closely at his defining beliefs and found that they were mostly about being insecure. He also saw that he compensated for his insecurities by being controlling and emotionally abusive.

Because of the devastating consequences of his previous behavior, Paul was motivated to change his beliefs about himself and the actions stemming from them. He worked hard at having more faith in himself and in treating others with kindness and respect. A few years later he entered into a relationship with a woman who was committed to also examining her defining beliefs and making the necessary changes. They held each other accountable for any lapses in behavior and ended up with a healthy, happy marriage.

Reading your own defining beliefs becomes easier when you learn to read the beliefs of people around you. When you see several instances of a certain behavior, you can usually spot a belief driving them. Using the technique of observing multiple contexts we talked about in Chapter 7, let's look at the actions of a woman named Jo to see if we can discern a governing belief in her life:

First context: Jo's father and mother divorced—and her father left town—when Jo was a teenager. She felt rejected by her dad, but she wanted to maintain a relationship with him, so she kept the lines of communication open between them.

Second context: In her twenties, Jo found herself in an emotionally-abusive marriage, which she left after eight years and two children. She worked to stay on friendly terms with her ex-husband so her children could have as stable an environment as possible under the circumstances.

Third context: Jo's grandmother wrote her a mean letter criticizing her for divorcing her husband. When someone asked Jo why she continued to visit and interact with her grandmother after receiving that letter, she said, "I don't want to carry hate in my heart. I know that would only hurt *me*."

Fourth context: In Jo's second marriage, she felt betrayed by certain actions of her stepdaughter, but she continued to show the girl love and support while still calling her on her behavior.

Can you see a governing belief emerge in the center of all these contexts? One way to state it might be: *Forgiveness is a Valuable Principle to Me.* Or it could be stated like this: *Relationships are More Important than Nursing Grievances.*

A DAUGHTER TELLS IT LIKE IT IS
Hayden tells the story of having his defining belief shown to him by his daughter:

"One day my little girl said to me, 'Daddy, why do you always say you'll do something, but you do something else?' I realized right then that my words were not congruent with my actions. My belief was that I could say what was convenient in the moment, but I didn't need to be committed to following through on my promises. I guess I believed that integrity was not important in my life. I decided to change that. From that point on I made a concerted effort to match my actions with my words."

Hayden read his own governing beliefs by looking at his actions. He had learned that technique by connecting other people's actions with their beliefs. The major indicator of the strength of your ability to read another person's governing beliefs is your accuracy in predicting their behavior. In other words, if you are correct when you guess what a person or group will do in the future, you are probably right about what they really believe. And one of the best ways to see real governing beliefs is to observe interactions between people, as we'll discuss in the next chapter.

The best way to read real beliefs is in an exchange.

You have more clarity when you can detach from the exchange.

9
The Secret Is In The Relationship

We do something every day without even realizing it: We participate in exchanges. We exchange money for goods and services; our expertise for a salary; time and energy for other things we want. Our relationships are also exchanges—we barter our love and loyalty for the affection and fidelity of another person. When we benefit in some way from a relationship, we continue the exchange.

ALL RELATIONSHIPS ARE EXCHANGES
If our Belief Window creates the role we play in life, and our Box is the stage on which we perform, Exchanges are the scripts we use. When we are in any kind of relationship—parent/child, husband/wife, boss/employee, or friendship—we ask for something or offer something, with the implicit understanding that the other person will reciprocate. All interactions operate this way, whether we recognize it or not.

We often enter into relationships without considering the cost involved. In other words, we don't analyze the equitability of the exchange. When the price of staying in a relationship is higher than what we perceive the benefits to be, we leave. If we stay in what seems to be an inequitable relationship, we are getting some kind of payoff; it just may not be obvious to an observer.

The Collapse of Belief

For example, the wife who stays in an abusive marriage might be getting the confirmation of her belief that she deserves to be treated that way. Or it is worth it to keep her family together. Or she may be frightened to be alone.

EXCHANGES ARE RUN BY BELIEFS

In any exchange, each party has his or her own principles or beliefs that govern the terms of the interaction. While it is easy to see the principles that apply in impersonal exchanges, such as financial transactions—buying a car or borrowing money, for example—it's harder to see the beliefs that govern the emotional exchanges we have with family and friends.

But no matter the relationship, the beliefs are always there, directing the interaction. They may be logical or silly, but either way, our beliefs run all our exchanges.

Here are some beliefs that might be discerned in exchanges:

- It's OK to blame others for my failures.
- My job is to make everyone around me happy.
- I need to be the center of attention.
- Our organization has the right to control your life.
- I cannot leave a situation until I have given everything in me.
- The parents' job is to do everything for their child.
- I am only obligated to be nice to people who do what I say.

Sometimes we are totally aware of the beliefs that run certain exchanges in our lives—and we state them to the other person, as you will see in the following story.

A TEENAGER WHO ACTUALLY CHANGED HIS BELIEF

Jared and his mom often have arguments about how they believe their relationship should work: Jared wants the best designer sneakers, all the latest video games, complete privacy in his room (which he never cleans) and no chores. He believes he deserves all this just for being a kid, and his mom is obligated to give it to him because "that's what moms are for."

Jared's mom has a different belief. She agrees that a parent is required to provide the basic necessities for a child's life, but if children want luxury and special privileges, they need to give something in return. So one day she sat Jared down and made a list of everything she did for him: good meals, extra nice clothes, driving him everywhere, laundry done, clean house, etc. She then asked, "What do I get in exchange for giving you all this?" Jared's mouth dropped open, and he stammered, "Whaaat?" Mom then explained the principle of exchanges and how the most successful ones are equitable. Jared was sobered by the conversation and soon began offering to do extra chores when he wanted special favors from his mom.

Sometimes the most important beliefs governing our exchanges are hidden. We aren't even aware of them. They are unspoken assumptions about what we expect of others. Unseen beliefs usually have more power over relationships than ones that are out in the open. They operate under the table, while the spoken beliefs, which ostensibly direct the relationship, are on the table, loudly proclaimed. But hidden beliefs invisibly control both parties in an exchange. Problems and conflicts in the relationship will continue as long as the beliefs remain hidden.

FORCED TO BE A SURROGATE MOM

April was the oldest child in a family of 10 children. Her father worked long hours to provide for the family and wasn't available to help with housework or childcare, so the mom used April as a babysitter, cook and housekeeper. April was not allowed to join any clubs in school or participate in extracurricular activities because she was always needed at home.

April's parents often told her they were building character in her by making her work so hard. But April had never agreed to the arrangement. It was imposed on her without her consent, and she got virtually nothing in return. She missed out on many normal childhood activities because of her enforced servitude.

This exchange was basically a con job, with a hidden agenda under the table. There was never any honest discussion between April and her parents to work out an equitable exchange.

When April was old enough, she left home at the earliest opportunity and went to college in a distant city. In later years, as she attempted to bring up what she considered her childhood abuse, her parents became more and more distant. They were not open to examining or exposing their hidden beliefs.

BELIEFS ARE HELD IN PLACE BY RELATIONSHIPS

The most important commodity exchanged within primary relationships is the validation of belief. For certain relationships to remain stable, both parties must share a common belief, which is promoted as unquestionably true. If one party stops believing the premise, the relationship will undergo stress and may even dissolve.

A typical scenario involving a common belief is that of religious conviction. A couple may enter into a marriage with the shared belief that their church is true, or at least the right one in which to raise their family. If one spouse subsequently decides that the religion is not an emotionally healthy place to be, the other could feel that the terms of their exchange have been violated, and may even terminate the relationship.

Another scenario is a business setting. If a CEO has his ego involved in being right about a project, he may subliminally insist that his team agree with him. If an underling points out serious flaws in the project, the CEO may kick him or her off the team, even if what was brought up was valid.

A third scenario might be friendship. Your buddy adamantly claims that he only does what is in your best interest. But if you ever have the nerve to suggest that pushing you to join his latest network marketing scheme is in *his* interest, not yours, he just might blow his top. You are not allowed to contradict the promoted belief in his exchange with you.

A rule is a belief applied to a specific exchange. When those rules are hidden, the exchange is warped and dysfunctional. If you can discover the hidden rules and expose them, *something* will change. The exchange might become more healthy, or it may fall apart completely—it depends on how disposed the participants are to owning up to their hidden agendas, of which they may not even be conscious.

WHEN YOUR BELIEFS CHANGE, RELATIONSHIPS WOBBLE

Your core beliefs define your value and create the structure that drives your life. That's why we call them defining or governing beliefs. They are held in place by the cables of your relationships. Many times, for a belief to change, certain exchanges have to be reset. Other times, when a belief changes *within* a relationship, it radically upsets the status quo.

You have many strings connected to you from all the people around you who expect you to be a certain way, good or bad. When you start moving, changing, those strings start wiggling. People everywhere are going to get nervous when your beliefs evolve. In fact, you may want to be prepared for all hell to break loose.

When you decide to change (or you have no choice), even if that change is for the better, it will rattle people in your life because you help hold their belief system in place. To minimize the impact on your close relationships as your beliefs evolve, a good strategy is to lie low for a while and resist the temptation to process your struggles with people you know won't be sympathetic. When you're more stable and grounded in your new beliefs, you can cautiously approach them with the news.

THE BEST WAY TO READ A BELIEF IS IN AN EXCHANGE

Beliefs are most easily read through the dynamics of an exchange. And if you can observe multiple exchanges with the same person or group, you will see a pattern emerge. It's kind of like mapping the location of a radio beacon. You have to take at least two readings from different places. The first reading gives the direction; the second gives the position. By combining both sets of data, you can home in on the source of the beacon.

The same is true of mapping governing beliefs. There is an underlying consistency in the pattern of interactions that becomes apparent when you take readings from several contexts. An operating belief will come into view when you watch actions instead of proclamations.

Discovering the real beliefs that drive behavior can be interesting. Some companies proclaim that they care about all their employees, but the pattern of their exchanges shows that only the people at the top are well-compensated, while the frontline employees are exploited.

Certain churches say they are family oriented and that their priority is to serve God. But their actions show them to be mainly focused on their image, controlling their members, and keeping the donation money flowing.

The Collapse of Belief

A person's relationship to and beliefs about power can be read in his or her exchanges.

A father may usurp power in an exchange with his daughter ...

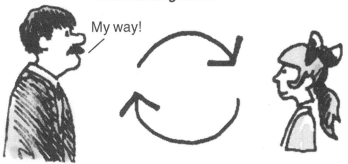

My way!

... but he may jockey for power in an exchange with a peer.

... but now it's going to be my way!

... or subordinate himself to powerful forces in the corporation he works for.

Whatever is best for the company.

A SUBTLE SHIFT IN PERCEPTION
Discerning a belief behind an exchange always changes *you*. Your perception shifts and you will never see the situation the same way again. You move from a place of buying into an expressed belief to a place of discerning the intention behind the action. You are starting to step out of The Box.

Barbara recently watched an exchange between two friends that helped her read their governing beliefs. Ruth asked Allen what he thought about a certain ethical principle, and Allen replied, "Well, the scriptures say …" Ruth cut him off and said, "I don't want to know what the Bible says, I want to know what *you* think about it." Allen hemmed and hawed for a few moments before he said, somewhat abashed, "You know, I don't really know what *I* think about that."

The beliefs of both parties became apparent to Barbara as she witnessed the interchange. She could see that Allen believed he didn't have to be introspective about spiritual principles; he only needed to adhere to what was said in his holy book and from the pulpit on Sunday. In other words, the thinking had been done, and he was off the hook.

Ruth, on the other hand, believed that we are all responsible for our own moral compasses, and can trust them. She is confident that our inner guidance is the highest source of truth, even higher than a written or spoken source revered by many.

PREDICTING THE FUTURE
I watched an exchange years ago between a young friend of mine and his employer. Alex was a computer whiz and was hired to work in a company that purported to be on the cutting edge of computer animation. He was thrilled with his job and excitedly told me about the promises his boss had made regarding his future in the company.

But something seemed off to me. I watched as the boss bought new cars and fancy furniture for the office, but kept Alex on a subsistence-level salary. There were also other little incongruities that seemed to say the boss was a user. I suspected he was taking advantage of Alex and would betray him in the end.

I tentatively voiced my concerns to Alex, but he waved them away, sure of his boss's good intentions. A few months later I saw Alex, and boy, had his tune changed. He was spitting mad!

The Collapse of Belief

His boss had bankrupted the company with his lavish spending and had left Alex hanging out to dry.

Alex's future was right there to see in the exchanges with his employer, but he was too emotionally involved to discern the pattern. Since I was more detached, it was easier for me to read the situation.

A promoted belief

A defining belief

SEEING BEHIND VALIDATIONS OF BELIEF

We tend to read relationships through our own Belief Window instead of the other party's Window. So we might read "love" there when it is absent, "commitment" when it is weak, or "honesty" when it doesn't exist. If we don't read beliefs accurately, their collapse brings much more pain than is necessary.

The greatest suffering we experience with the collapse of belief is in our relationships, as we've said before. A collapse can damage our relationship to people, places, institutions, money, and so on. But if we can observe situations and exchanges with some degree of detachment, looking for clues that show governing beliefs, we can lessen or avoid altogether a lot of misery and trauma.

Sometimes we can be pleasantly surprised by what we see. The loyalty and integrity of my former business partner, Larry, reveals a Belief Window that has never disappointed me. His actions have always been consistent with his words, and we're still friends after many years.

But when someone unexpectedly turns on you, after you get over the shock, look back. You will probably see that the indications were there all along if you had known how to look for them. It is much less painful to see a dangerous Belief Window beforehand rather than getting caught in the drama when everything goes down.

Sharon had a business partner, Hillary, whom she admired and looked up to. Hillary had strong intuitive abilities that greatly impressed Sharon, who created a Belief Window that said *My Partner Can Do No Wrong.* For a while their business thrived, and then one day Hillary announced that she was transferring all the company's intellectual property into a corporation that only she owned. Sharon was surprised and disappointed, but still held on firmly to her Belief Window about her partner.

Sharon's husband encouraged her to look at the situation without the filter of her belief about Hillary. He pointed out the inconsistency of Hillary's actions with her words. His perspective gave Sharon permission to drop her Belief Window and consider the raw facts. She finally saw Hillary for what she really was: an imperfect person who, through fear, was grasping for whatever she could get to increase her security.

The business eventually began to fail, and Sharon and Hillary decided to divide it up and go their separate ways. When Hillary refused to allow Sharon even temporary access to the intellectual property she needed to continue operating her half of the company, Sharon could see that her latter discernment about Hillary was correct.

A LITTLE LESS IDEALISTIC

I have seen many people go through a collapse of belief. The most excruciating type is usually a loss of faith in their religion. One of the greatest losses they feel in that scenario is in discovering that their loved ones are more loyal to the church than they are to them or their relationship. But that had always been the case—they just hadn't read it.

So our advice to you is to be a little less idealistic and a little more discerning. It is easier to look realistically at a scenario when the sun is shining than to wait and discover the truth during a storm.

We all have idealistic beliefs, big and small, collapsing all the time. Sometimes we face the devastation and deal with it, but many times we do not—we don't want to pay the price of letting a belief go. But not facing the truth brings an even higher cost: self deception and duplicity. If we continue to deny reality, the only way to keep holding onto a collapsed belief is insanity or death.

**WHEN
THE HEAD
IS ON
STRAIGHT**
. . . the heart can heal

10
Beyond Belief

When I was a very young boy, my mother showed me something on our walks around our ranch. She pointed to marks on the ground and told me that by looking carefully at the patterns in the soft dust, I could tell what kind of animal had been there. For some reason, that information had a profound effect on me. I became fascinated with reading patterns, from tracks in the dirt to themes in my life. Throughout my youth and into adulthood I observed my world closely and became adept at interpreting patterns, not only in nature, but in people and situations as well.

Early in my career as an industrial designer I found myself drawn to information design. I began to see the patterns in information—and how seemingly unrelated fields are linked in ways that are not apparent at first glance. In my work as a museum designer I had to find a way to quickly assimilate mounds of information from many disciplines. Because I am dyslexic, the best way for me to process is visually, so I developed a system I called Relational Thinking that graphically portrays the connections between different subjects and contexts.

As I refined the Relational Thinking system I could see its application in many areas. It was instrumental in helping me design the numerous museum exhibits and visitors' centers I worked on, and it helped me create over 30 books. I also used it to teach art and design at Brigham Young University. The more I got into the process, the more I could see the links between contexts and the underlying paradigms that drive behavior.

I eventually renamed the process Paradigm Mapping because I found that the paradigms inherent in every situation influence not only that context, but many things related to it. This understanding led me into business consulting and even life coaching, using Paradigm Mapping to solve complex problems for my clients. Barbara and I later developed a series of workshops in which we teach the steps of the system and give the participants practice using the process.

ANOTHER WORD FOR BELIEF
A paradigm is just another name for a belief, and mapping your paradigms can help you take conscious control of them. Our beliefs control our perception, as we said earlier, and there is a definite link between perception and choice.

The key to Paradigm Mapping is to extract the core principle or idea from a situation, and then link it to multiple contexts. This brings new perspectives and insights. The system was so successful in my art classes at BYU, I wanted to experiment with other subjects. So I teamed up with a history professor to use the process to teach American History to multicultural students.

As we connected the paradigms and principles in U.S. history and the Constitution to other disciplines and subjects, we also required the students to apply each principle to their own lives. They struggled with assimilating knowledge in this strange way, but after about 30 times through the process, something interesting would always happen: It was like a light would go on in their minds, and they started seeing connections everywhere. They began to relate the principles we discussed in class to practical, everyday events in their lives.

For example, one day, as we were discussing the reconstruction of the South after the Civil War, a Japanese girl in the front row began to weep. When asked what the matter was, she explained that after years of a stressful relationship with her husband's family, she finally understood what was going on. That day in class she made the connection between the carpetbaggers who came to the defeated southern states—saying they were there to help the people, but in reality taking advantage of them—and her mother-in-law, who packaged her deep self-interest and manipulation in pious religious talk. Her beliefs about the scenario changed from that moment on. She was no longer an unwilling participant in her mother-in-law's Box; she could see the situation for what it was and take steps to protect herself.

Understanding the holistic nature of life seemed to have a profound effect on the students in those history classes. They developed a unity that was deep and sincere. I saw Palestinians and Israelis embrace. Kids from all over the world started to have interconnected dreams. (Even the other professor and I did.) The course was taught that way for eight years to over 1400 students, and the results were always the same—astonishing insights into life, and deep bonds between the students.

The kids in the class had been ripped out of their home culture and had to assimilate a lot of new contexts in a short amount of time. In that history class we took them through even more contexts academically. We discovered that once we taught the paradigm-mapping process, we couldn't fix its boundaries; we never knew where it would go. One of the most surprising comments the students constantly made was, "Why is it that we never talk of God in this course, but I see God everywhere now?" This comment always shocked us because we were very careful to never bring up religion in any way; we didn't want to get in trouble with the administration. But the process seemed to give the students a hint about a universal connecting energy of some kind.

THERE ARE THINGS YOU CANNOT KNOW DIRECTLY

I came to realize that there are certain things that cannot be known directly; but that by dancing the dance through multiple contexts we can begin to comprehend the unknowable. When we operate from only one perspective, such as a purely scientific or a purely religious context, our perception is warped and our judgment is skewed; we don't see the whole picture. When we only have one view, we only have one choice. The relentless imposition of one point of view has been catastrophic for this planet.

Another unexpected consequence of teaching history with paradigm mapping was that many students in the class bailed out of BYU. They began to read the control issues inherent in a reli-

The Collapse of Belief

giously-affiliated institution and transferred out in surprising numbers.

The process of paradigm mapping is what finally cracked my belief in organized religion. I resisted bringing the process into my personal life for as long as I could, but it eventually went where it needed to go. I'll never forget the day I set my relational material and academic books next to my church books and watched my beliefs collapse. The fallout extended to my marriage and many other family relationships. This process can be dangerous, but it takes you to where some deeper part of yourself really wants to be.

FOUNDATIONAL CONCEPTS

The foundational concepts of Paradigm Mapping, as they relate to belief, can be summed up in three statements:

1. *I am where I am in life largely because of the choices I have made.*
2. *Most of these life-positioning choices are made because of my beliefs.*
3. *The most powerful beliefs directing my choices are the beliefs about myself.*

Your defining beliefs or governing paradigms can usually be simply stated and are often constructed subconsciously in childhood. They can be unknown to you and are always expressed within the exchanges in your relationships. Defining beliefs are hierarchical in nature, radiating outward and influencing virtually every decision you make.

Your promoted beliefs are those beliefs of which you are consciously aware. When contradictions to your promoted beliefs occur, the resulting internal conflict causes a split between your idealized self and its exaggerated opposite (your hidden defining belief, or shadow). This cognitive dissonance can cause you to manipulate your perception to see only the idealized self and deny the existence of the shadow self. If you cannot face the discrepancy between the two and resolve it, you will need to become duplicitous in your exchanges with others in order to validate your idealized model of yourself and subtly invalidate its opposite. You will begin to orchestrate situations to discount, separate from, or destroy contradictions to your idealized beliefs, and project onto others the characteristics of your shadow. The more duplicitous and self-deceptive you become, the more you will invest time, attention and resources into your self-validation efforts.

This relentless promotion of your idealized beliefs, hiding your defining beliefs even from yourself, will result in double-bind situations that you see no way out of, and poor discernment where you need it the most. Your choices will become more and more warped as you attempt to reconcile the conflict between your idealized self and your darker hidden self. You can stumble along in this dysfunction your entire life, or at some point, a catastrophic event or other devastating situation can cause a collapse of your idealized beliefs.

If you'd rather avoid the trauma of the above scenario, you can circumvent much of the distress by creating a perceptual shift: you can *make your belief-building process conscious.* This will result in enhanced discernment and more accurate perception. As you become aware of how beliefs are formed you will begin to discover the underlying rules that control the exchanges of life. You will become proficient at pattern reading and skilled at adapting to totally new situations. You may even surprise yourself at how well you can predict the future.

ADAPTABILITY AND FLEXIBILITY
HAVE NEVER BEEN MORE IMPORTANT
The world around us is changing at an exponential rate. You are going to need the ability to adjust to and control the rapid collapse of invalid belief structures, and the ability to create new, more workable beliefs. By doing so, you can transcend the dysfunctional systems and double-bind situations in which you find yourself.

The most significant thing Paradigm Mapping will show you is your own defining beliefs. The next most significant thing you will see is the governing paradigms or beliefs of people around you. Then you will begin to recognize the beliefs that drive all kinds of exchanges in all sorts of relationships.

Beliefs can get us moving, but they can also imprison us. Once we understand how our beliefs are created, and that they can be temporary and dynamic, avenues to adapting open up. When a formerly abused child, for example, becomes aware of the origin of her defining belief that *My Purpose in Life is to be Used*

The Collapse of Belief

by Others, she is able to consciously change it to *I Am Worth being Treated with Respect and Kindness.*

THE ANSWERS ARE OUTSIDE THE BOX

The most important concept you can learn from this book is that the solutions to your problems are invariably outside your Box of Belief. As long as you stay inside your Box's belief-dictating parameters you can never see—much less accept—any resolution that may be just across that barrier. A conscious awareness and active involvement in your belief-building process reduces or eliminates the pain and suffering experienced by a collapsing belief. You can instead celebrate the *evolution* of belief. Accepting the inaccuracies within your defining beliefs is the key to having power over the predicaments in which you find yourself.

The best tool we have to get out of our Boxes is discernment. Your ability to recognize and respond to even subtle shifts in your environment will increase as you learn to analyze your beliefs and those of others. Take note that one of the most damaging by-products of an unquestioned belief system is diminished discernment.

But discernment can be a bitch, if you'll pardon the expression. It can be painful to put aside what you want to believe and *read* the situation. I'll never forget consulting with a certain company from which money had been embezzled. Until the owner was willing to consider all possibilities, including that the thief might even be his own son (which it turned out to be), the mystery of the missing funds could not be solved. Since I was an outsider, with no emotional investment in the outcome, I could see more clearly, and was able to pinpoint the problem fairly quickly.

Sometimes all that is needed to topple an erroneous belief system is just a tiny piece of information from a different viewpoint. Here are a couple of stories that illustrate that principle:

The oppressed citizens of North Korea are constantly told how much better off they are than their capitalist neighbors in the South. But the merest sliver of real news was enough to fracture the illusion of well-being for Kim Tae Jin, a North Korean defector. He saw a photograph of what were said to be impoverished and oppressed South Korean workers. Some of them were wearing jackets with zippers, and one had a ballpoint pen in his pocket—both unheard-of luxuries in North Korea. Kim saw through the lies in one flash of shocked awareness.

Years ago, during the Soviet reign in eastern Europe, a visiting diplomat from that region had his belief in the superiority of communism collapse when he entered an American supermarket. He thought the store was fake at first. "If it were real," he said, "there would be long lines of people to buy all that food." But when he instructed his driver to take him across town to another store not on the planned route, he saw the same thing, and his conviction cracked.

It is a constant struggle to detach from our emotions and just *look*. I work at it every day, and when I am successful, people ask me how I see things others don't. I respond that it's simple: I'm the only one looking; everyone else is promoting or posturing. One of the most profound insights I ever received was realizing that most of our time is spent confirming our beliefs, assuring ourselves that we're right. We spend very little time examining our beliefs.

You can only see your world accurately when you set aside your Belief Window.

A FEW CLOSING POINTS
The world is an interesting and dynamic place. We would appreciate it more if we weren't so consumed with shoring up our belief systems. We all, at one time or another, get stuck in a Box—either our own or someone else's—frantically searching the same ground again and again for a solution we never find. In order to find answers, survive and even thrive in this tumultuous world, we must take responsibility for our beliefs. It is pos-

sible to become aware of our defining beliefs and make choices based on reality—leaving behind our confining Boxes and limiting Belief Windows. Here are five steps in that direction we have offered in this book:

1. *Understand what beliefs really are (constructions of your mind) and how you build them (by your interpretation of events and interactions).*
2. *Learn to turn off and on the need to validate your beliefs.*
3. *Discern hidden beliefs through the pattern of exchanges.*
4. *Step outside your Box and set aside your Belief Window, if only temporarily, and look objectively at the facts from several viewpoints.*
5. *Realize that this is one of the most difficult challenges life can throw at you, so give yourself time to process.*

THE POWER OF BELIEF

Beliefs have caused the largest enslavement of the human race—whether they are hidden behind a cross, a corporate spreadsheet or a political slogan. Rigid, immovable belief systems are responsible for monumental disasters. 9/11, the Holocaust, and the banking and mortgage failures of 2008 are prominent examples.

But beliefs are also responsible for some of the greatest achievements of humankind. The belief in a faster route to the Far East drove Columbus's voyage. The belief that we can solve problems through science resulted in great advances in medicine and technology. Beliefs have driven the highest human achievements, and they are also the basis for the lowest levels of human depravity. Beliefs can help us reach our dreams, but they can also bind us in chains. Their effects can be seen from the loftiness of the Sistine Chapel and missions to the moon, to the blood-soaked streets of countries yearning for freedom.

Beliefs are not perfect and unchangeable. How can imperfect humans build perfect beliefs? Changing beliefs can actually promote progress and growth. As you become aware of your defining beliefs and how they do or do not serve you, you will come to see change, even collapse, as an opportunity—a chance for new beginnings.

When your beliefs collapse, you will be shown who you really are. You may discover a rod of steel inside you that you never knew was there. You will be surprised at your courage. That which is at your center is what truly defines you. You are more than you think you are. You are also part of something much bigger and more intricate than you can imagine.

There is a place we all visit from time to time that is beyond belief: When we are caught up in the moment—engrossed in a sports activity, wrapped in the arms of a lover, looking into the eyes of a child—we are not validating our beliefs nor projecting them onto anyone else. We are not agonizing over the past or fearing the future; we are savoring the present, with no boxes or windows clouding our sight.

Perhaps we should go to that place more often.

ACKNOWLEDGMENTS

We are indebted to many people who helped bring this book into being. Jeff Ricks, the founder of PostMormon.org, created a forum for the ideas we presented here to be shared in the first place. The feedback we received from the members of that discussion group encouraged us to consider compiling our ideas into a book. Karen and Liz's brutally honest technical and conceptual criticism was much appreciated, and caused us to rewrite the book several times. Thanks also to Max Crapo, Candy Eyerly, Marianne Berrett, Glenn Beck (the other one), Paul Allen, Alecia, Amy Cox, and many others from Postmo, whom we only know by their avatars, for their supportive responses to this material.

We have wonderful friends who patiently read several versions of the manuscript and gave us valuable advice: Ron and Cathy Phillips, Dave and Michelle Gray, and Rain Sundberg were key. The flow and content of this book would have suffered without their insightful suggestions. We especially appreciated their help in fleshing out certain areas that lacked clarification.

Thanks, guys. We couldn't have done it without you!

PM CORE PROCESS DIAGRAM

1 *IDENTIFY the GENERATING CONTEXT.*
This is the context (situation or subject) within which you apply the process.

2 *READ the PATTERNS.*
From that context, extract an underlying rule or principle.

3 *STATE the RULE or PRINCIPLE*
with generalized words and simple images.

4 *LINK to OTHER CONTEXTS.*
List other areas where this principle shows up.

5 *SEE the expression in your OWN LIFE.*
The most important context is your own life–linking the principle to something that is yours.

Generating Context → **Principle or Rule** *See notes on next page* → Own Context, Other Context, Other Context, Other Context

Multiple Contexts
Any context can be used – history, geology, English, chemistry, organizational behavior, cooking, archaeology, marketing, law, psychology, agriculture, film, Uncle Elbert's closet, etc.

Paradigm Mapping

The Paradigm Mapping system described in Chapter 10 is the underlying process we used to create this book. The diagram at left illustrates the components of the system. PM teaches you to see hidden elements that affect situations and interactions in your world. It provides understanding and tools that improve your problem-solving abilities and overall life skills. Paradigm Mapping also enhances predictive capabilities, which will help you adapt to evolving and rapidly-changing conditions.

NOTES ON THE DIAGRAM:

***Crucial Elements of the Principle or Rule**
 1. A principle or rule is always stated in terms of a relationship between elements or parts. (Example: "It rains" is not a principle. "It rains when clouds reach a saturation point" is a principle.)
 2. State the principle in general terms in order to apply it to several contexts. Use multiple modes of expression--visual, verbal, dance, etc. – to employ more areas of the brain.

Advantages of Relating Across Multiple Contexts
In the process of relating or connecting one idea to another, you can see what was unseen before.

Special Note: As your discernment becomes sharper, the barriers between this dimension and others can actually begin to dissolve.

For more information about Paradigm Mapping, visit: www.KurtHanks.com

Made in the USA
Lexington, KY
19 April 2013